ENDORSEMENTS

R.C. Sproul has an amazing gift for explaining difficult truths in pithy, memorable, and easy-to-grasp ways. He is the ideal teacher for a study of the Lord's Prayer, because the prayer itself is a profound lesson on a difficult subject, given by Jesus to His disciples in an amazing economy of words. You will be greatly blessed and edified by this book.

—Dr. John MacArthur
Pastor-teacher
Grace Community Church
Sun Valley, California

Here is a very special book on prayer. It will not leave you overwhelmed with failure and crushed into "giving prayer yet another try"—as many books and sermons on prayer do. Instead, it will lead you gently by the hand—as Jesus did when He taught the disciples the prayer on which these pages are based. It will draw you into a sense of the privilege of prayer, stimulate new desires to pray, even leave you with a sense of the delights of prayer. These pages have an atmosphere of light and are permeated by a sense of freshness and joy. Happy indeed is the theologian who can stimulate prayer. And happy are we that R.C. Sproul is such a theologian. *The Prayer of the Lord* is—quite simply—a spiritual treat.

—Dr. Sinclair B. Ferguson
Teaching Fellow
Ligonier Ministries

I love listening to R.C. Sproul teach, and this book sounds just like him—penetrating truths strikingly illustrated. His good quotations and pastoral wisdom make him as easy to read as he is delightful to listen to (and the short chapters help!). Sproul clearly explains the Scriptures with sentences that are simple and accurate. He knows enough to say important things concisely and clearly—truths about the kingdom, the fatherhood of God, history, and, of course, prayer. There's even a helpful question-and-answer section at the end. This little book now takes its place with the classics on prayer.

—Dr. Mark Dever
Senior pastor
Capitol Hill Baptist Church
Washington, D.C.

Gospel-driven disciple-making in the church has historically made full use of the Apostles' Creed, the law of God, and the Lord's Prayer. Now through this marvelous and insightful exposition of the Lord's Prayer, R.C. has provided disciple-making Christians and churches with an excellent and useful instrument to direct and fulfill the heart's desire of every believer who would cry out, "Lord, teach us to pray."

—Dr. Harry L. Reeder III
Senior pastor
Briarwood Presbyterian Church
Birmingham, Alabama

The Prayer of the Lord

THE

Prayer

OF THE

Lord

R.C. SPROUL

IR *Reformation Trust* A DIVISION OF LIGONIER MINISTRIES, ORLANDO, FL

The Prayer of the Lord
© Copyright 2009 by R.C. Sproul

Published by Reformation Trust Publishing
a division of Ligonier Ministries
421 Ligonier Court, Sanford, FL 32771
Ligonier.org   ReformationTrust.com

Printed in Ann Arbor, Michigan
Cushing-Malloy, Inc.
April 2018
First edition, first paperback printing

978-1-56769-994-4 (Paperback)
978-1-64289-003-7 (ePub)
978-1-64289-004-4 (Kindle)

Cover design: Vanessa Wingo
Interior design and typeset: Katherine Lloyd, The DESK

Scripture taken from the *New King James Version*®. Copyright © 1982 by
Thomas Nelson. Used by permission. All rights reserved.

Library of Congress Cataloging-in-Publication Data

Sproul, R. C. (Robert Charles), 1939-2017
    The prayer of the Lord / R.C. Sproul.
        p. cm.
    Includes indexes.
    ISBN 978-1-56769-118-4
    1. Lord's prayer--Criticism, interpretation, etc. 2. Prayer--Reformed Church.
I. Title.
    BV230.S65 2009
    226.9'6077--dc22

                                                        2009001247

To the people of Saint Andrew's Chapel
in Sanford, Florida

CONTENTS

ONE

How Not to Pray

A few years ago, when I happened to be in San Diego for a conference, I unexpectedly ran into an old friend of mine, George Miladin. George is a pianist and a master teacher—he used to host a televised teaching program for the piano called the "See and Hear Piano Series." Seeing George again presented me with a golden opportunity, so after one of the plenary sessions of the conference, I grabbed George and said, "Let's go find a piano." So we looked through the church until we found a choir rehearsal room, and we went in there and closed the door. I said to George, "Teach me some things about the piano," because I love to play the piano and learn new little things. So George, the master teacher, sat down at the piano and showed me a couple of little techniques that he uses in his repertoire.

I thought about that afterward, about how eager I was to get George aside so that he could teach me to do something I didn't know how to do. I will go out of my way to ask a person to teach me something if I have great admiration for his ability or prowess in a particular skill or art, particularly if it's something I'm interested in.

There was a point during the earthly ministry of Jesus when His disciples had the opportunity to do the same thing I did with my friend George. They had the opportunity to ask the Master Teacher to teach them something. Of course, Jesus had been teaching them on a daily basis for some time already. Each of them had enrolled in His school, becoming a *mathetes*, a "learner" or "student." They enrolled when Jesus said to them, "Follow Me." When He said that, He meant it literally. His school wasn't housed in a building and it didn't feature a regular schedule of classes. Jesus was a rabbi who had a peripatetic ministry; that is, He moved about from village to village, and His disciples went with Him, forming an entourage of sorts. When Jesus called the disciples, He wasn't just saying, "Follow my teachings." He literally wanted them to follow Him. So these men gathered about Jesus and walked behind Him, trying to memorize the teaching He gave them as they walked along the roads. Obviously they got more than they bargained for. Not only did they learn the great truths of the Scriptures by following after Jesus, they also were given the unspeakable privilege of being eyewitnesses of the multitude of miracles that Jesus performed.

Imagine what it must have been like to have the privilege of following Jesus around day after day, listening to His teaching and watching Him perform His miracles. I can think of lots of things they could have asked Him to teach them. The disciples might have gone to Him and said, "Jesus, teach us how to turn the water into wine." They might have asked, "Teach us how to walk on the water." Or they could have said, "Teach us how to raise people from the dead." Those are the kinds of questions I would have asked Him. But the New Testament tells us of a different request that the disciples brought to Jesus. They came to Him on one occasion, as Luke records it for us in his Gospel, and said, "Lord, teach us to pray" (Luke 11:1b). I find it fascinating that this was the burning question they brought to Jesus. They wanted to gain a special insight into prayer as a skill or an art.

The Master's Prayer Life

Why did they ask Him this question? My guess is that they saw the link between Jesus' extraordinary prayer life and His power, His teaching, His character, His whole person. They must have noticed that after ministering to large crowds of people, Jesus often would withdraw by Himself. He must have felt drained from that ministry. During such times, Jesus would not simply withdraw for a half hour or so. Rather, He would go apart for long periods, and when He did so, He usually spent much of the time in intense seasons of prayer. We know of the intensity of His prayer in the Garden of Gethsemane, when He prayed with such stress and fervency that His sweat was like great drops of blood. We know that before He selected His disciples and called them to follow after Him, He spent the entire night alone in prayer. The disciples could not help but notice this commitment to prayer. They saw the intimacy Jesus had with the Father and made the connection between His prayer and His power.

So they came to Jesus asking, "Lord, teach us to pray." And they added a little statement to that: ". . . as John also taught his disciples" (Luke 11:1c). They not only had noticed Jesus' extraordinary character, they also had seen it in John the Baptist and in John's followers, many of whom had transferred their devotion to Christ after John had pointed to Him.

I'm not only surprised that the disciples brought this particular request to Jesus, I'm a little bit surprised by how He responded. Far be it from me to suggest that He could have given a better answer. I simply would have thought Jesus would have said to His disciples, "If you really want to learn how to pray, immerse yourselves in the Psalms," because in the book of Psalms we have a collection of prayers that were given under the inspiration of God the Holy Spirit. As the New Testament tells us, the Holy Spirit is active in assisting us in our praying. We're not all that adept at prayer; it is a practice very few of us have mastered. We find it difficult to articulate our deepest feelings and our deepest concerns to God. Yet God is pleased to give His Holy Spirit to assist us in expressing ourselves to the Father in prayer. And He did that, obviously, for the psalmists of the Old Testament.

I've also been interested in some of the evaluations of church historians, which have showed that during those periods when the church flourished, when great spiritual vitality became manifest, and when worship reached its apogee—in short, during periods of special renewal—the Psalms were at the heart and center of the liturgy of the church and the devotional life of the people. Clearly, those who learn to meditate deeply on the Psalms experience the supreme Old Testament model of prayer that is provoked by God the Holy Spirit. So I would suggest that if you really want to learn how to pray and to discover the kinds of prayers that are pleasing to God, you should immerse yourselves in the Psalms.

Avoiding Hypocritical Practices

That wasn't how Jesus answered the disciples' question. Instead, He gave them what we now refer to as the Lord's Prayer, not because it was a prayer He Himself prayed, but because it was the prayer He provided for His followers. But before He gave the prayer, He made some prefatory remarks that we must not miss. In Matthew's account of the giving of the Lord's Prayer, which is recorded as part of the Sermon on the Mount, Jesus first said to His disciples:

> "When you pray, you shall not be like the hypocrites. For they love to pray standing in the synagogues and on the corners of the streets, that they may be seen by men. Assuredly, I say to you, they have their reward. But you, when you pray, go into your room, and when you have shut your door, pray to your Father who is in the secret place; and your Father who sees in secret, will reward you openly. And when you pray, do not use vain repetitions as the heathen do. For they think that they will be heard for their many words." (Matt. 6:5–7)

The disciples were looking for instructions on how to pray, but the first thing Jesus chose to tell them was how *not* to pray.

In these verses, He laid down two restrictions on prayer, and we need to take these restrictions seriously because God is neither honored nor pleased by prayer of the type Jesus addressed here.

The first type of prayer Jesus condemned is hypocritical prayer. The term *hypocrisy* in the New Testament is drawn from the culture of the day, where a hypocrite was one who engaged in drama, in the theater. He was play-acting. What he was doing was not real. So the original meaning of the term had nothing to do with insincerity—we don't charge actors today with being hypocrites or insincere simply because they're playing a role that does not correspond to their real lives. But Jesus applied the word to people who were going through the motions of prayer, making a great external show of piety, but whose real state did not match this outward show. Their piety was a sham; it was phony and fraudulent. It was a fake form of godliness, one that had been mastered by the Pharisees. Prayer, for them, was a business. Prayer was something that was expected from people in their positions, so they made a public display of their piety.

When I was a seminary student, I had the unfortunate experience of attending a school that was in its first year after the merger of two seminaries, and the new administration was committed to turning the seminary into a theological university rather than a typical divinity school. The administrators had lofty goals for the school's academic excellence. We students were the guinea pigs for that, before the administrators were able to make certain corrections. While I was in seminary, we were required to write term papers exceeding two hundred pages per year. And our reading lists were so large that we would go through and read the first line of each paragraph of the book in order to meet the requirements. I remember writing a twenty-page report on a book I hadn't even read, and I received an "A" for my effort. I had been a philosophy major, and this was a book by Martin Buber. I had studied Buber's existential philosophy, so I just assumed that, in this book, he applied his existential philosophy to theology, and I criticized him for that. But, as I said, I didn't read the book—that was the kind of thing we had to do to get through those assignments.

What I thought to be the worst assignment was in my sociology of religion class, where we were required to write a twenty-page paper analyzing the image of the minister in contemporary culture. We were required to leaf through magazines and the comic pages of the newspapers to find images of ministers and to observe how ministers were portrayed on television and in the movies. When we got that assignment and walked out the door, we began to sing spontaneously, "M-I-C-K-E-Y M-O-U-S-E." This was an assignment that we considered "Mickey Mouse," hardly worthy of our time.

Yet, to my utter astonishment, when I did the study for that paper, I made a discovery that comes back to my mind every time I see a minister portrayed on television or in the movies. I found that, far and wide, the minister is caricatured in our culture today, first, as something of a sourpuss, one whose lips are pursed and who has an aura of superiority about him, and second, as something of a wimp, a man lacking in masculinity. That image is transferred from the minister to Christians in general, so that believers are regarded as practicing a holier-than-thou posture.

During that time in seminary, I was grateful when a golf

course opened near my home and the owner invited me to play there on a ministerial discount, even though I wasn't yet ordained, but was serving as a student pastor in a nearby church. But it so happened that when I came in and signed up, the person behind the counter looked at me and said, "You don't look like a minister." I said, "Really? What is a minister supposed to look like?" I don't remember his answer, but whatever it was, I didn't fit his image—and I was supremely grateful for that in light of this caricature that is rampant in our culture.

A Façade of Hypocrisy

Where did this caricature come from? I'm afraid that it has come about because ministers far too often adopt the posture that Jesus teaches us to avoid—the posture that makes us appear to think we are holier than everyone around us. This posture is a façade of hypocrisy. Hypocrisy has a devastating impact on the life of the church and on the representation of Christianity to a dying world. And so our Lord warns us here not to parade our piety before the world.

We need to be careful here, because we Christians are enjoined to bear witness to our faith, which means making the invisible visible. But sometimes we think that one of the primary ways of bearing witness to people is by demonstrating our Christian spirituality with public prayer. That's dangerous, because the motivation for prayer is not to display our spirituality before the watching world. Prayer is to be intensely private. That's not to say that Christianity is to be private. I've heard people on talk shows say, "I never talk about my religion because religion is intensely personal and private." Well, I grant half of that thesis. Certainly, Christianity is personal. But it is not private. The New Testament gives us all kinds of mandates to declare our faith publicly. There is no such thing as a closet Christian; we're to bear witness to the world of our commitment to Christ and not hide it. However, prayer involves a special kind of communion. It is part of the special relationship between God and a believer individually or the church corporately. It is not meant to show anything about the person who prays.

I don't know how many times I've been in a worship service and I've heard the minister pray the pastoral prayer in such a way that I've wondered to whom he was speaking. When that happens, you get the strange sensation that the minister isn't talking to God but to those of us in the congregation. He's got us there as a captive audience, our eyes are closed, we're being quiet, and we're trying to focus on what he's saying, but we really should be eavesdropping, as it were, on the pastor as he is addressing God for us. He is representing us before the presence of God; that means his words are not for our ears primarily. But if he is not speaking consciously to God, he is not praying properly.

Just as Jesus warned against praying publicly in a hypocritical fashion, He also encouraged private prayer. He said, "Go into your closet, shut the door, and get on your face before God, and the Father who hears you in secret will reward you in public." God is not interested in our public displays of piety. He's not interested in religion in terms of the outward show. He's interested in godliness. Our spiritual lives are means to the end of godliness, and prayer is one of the key aspects of our spirituality.

Avoiding Pagan Practices

The second kind of prayer Jesus condemned is pagan prayer. He said: "And when you pray, do not use vain repetitions as the heathen do. For they think that they will be heard for their many words." Jesus was saying here that we must not regard prayer as some kind of magical incantation, for that is how pagans pray. They recite certain phrases over and over again, with no understanding of what the words mean. In these contexts, prayers are used as mantras, with the hope that they will change the environment or the circumstances in which a person lives. New Age thinking is filled with this type of thing. Jesus did not commend such exercises as godly forms of prayer; rather, He linked the use of vain repetitions to paganism.

Christians can easily fall into a pattern of praying in a repetitious fashion, without engaging their minds. It bothers me sometimes when Christians gather for a meal and the host will say to someone there, "John, will you please say the grace for us?" The host doesn't ask for someone to lead in prayer but to say the grace. That kind of language suggests a mere recitation, not a prayer that comes from the heart.

We can even treat the Lord's Prayer this way. The Lord's Prayer is an integral part of the worship of multitudes of Christians. Worship services often include the recitation of the Lord's Prayer. The use of the Lord's Prayer has a rich history in the church, and whenever we pray it or hear it, we are reminded of those priorities that Jesus sets before us as objects for prayer. Don't get me wrong—I'm not opposed to the recitation of the Lord's Prayer. However, there is a danger that this use of the prayer may be nothing *more* than a recitation. The praying of the Lord's Prayer can become as mindless and as vain a repetition as the magical incantations and mantras that pagans use.

Jesus did not give the Lord's Prayer with the intention that it would be repeated mindlessly. When we pray the Lord's Prayer, we need to pray it thoughtfully, giving attention in our minds to its content. It is not a mantra to be repeated without the engagement of the mind or heart. It is an example of godly prayer.

Of course, repetition has great value. I've often said that one of my favorite liturgies in the life of the church is the traditional marriage ceremony. You've heard it many times: "Dearly beloved, we are gathered together here today in the presence of God and of these witnesses to unite this man and this woman in the holy bonds of marriage, which was instituted by God," and so it goes. It's a very brief service. It contains pledges, vows, charges, and prayers. For me, the more often I lead this liturgy or hear it, the more blessed I am by the content of it. That is, the more familiar I become with the language, the more I think about it and meditate on it, and I see afresh how rich it is in explaining to us the sanctity of marriage. So it is with the Lord's Prayer. Hearing it over and over again may lead us to mindless repetition, but it also may burn these words, and the underlying principles, into our minds. Repetition in and of itself is not a bad thing. In fact, it's one of the most important ingredients of learning, because it's the rare person who masters a concept or a principle by hearing it once.

There was a great piano teacher who was teaching one of his students scales, and the student was bored to tears. The student said: "I don't want to play scales. I want to play like Van

Cliburn. I want to play like a great piano virtuoso." The teacher replied: "You know, you may never be able to play the piano like Van Cliburn; in fact, in all probability you won't be able to master this instrument to the degree that he has. But there is one thing you *can* do like Van Cliburn." The student asked, "What's that?" And the teacher said, "You can play your scales." Then he added: "Don't ever think that Van Cliburn became Van Cliburn without doing the scales over and over again so that those tones became second nature to him."

That's the benefit of praying a prayer like the Lord's Prayer over and over again. It becomes part of the fabric of our thinking. It begins to become a part of our souls, so that we fall back on it when we're at a loss as to how we ought to pray. We can always pray the Lord's Prayer.

Praying to the God Who Already Knows

After warning His disciples against hypocritical prayer and pagan prayer, Jesus went on to say, "Therefore do not be like them. For your Father knows the things you have need of before you ask Him" (Matt. 6:8). With these words, Jesus echoed the thoughts of David, who wrote: "O Lord, You have searched me and known me. You know my sitting down and my rising up; You understand my thought afar off. You comprehend my path and my lying down, and are acquainted with all my ways. For there is not a word on my tongue, but behold, O Lord, You know it altogether" (Ps. 139:1–4). Jesus is simply seconding the psalmist's affirmation that the Lord knows what we need before we ask it.

One of the most frequently asked questions in the theology of prayer is, "Does prayer change things?" The answer is evident. The New Testament makes it clear that prayer changes all kinds of things. We'll explore that issue more deeply later, but the next question that comes is, "Does prayer change God's mind?"

What would induce God to change His mind? Perhaps new information, some knowledge He lacks until we communicate it to Him for His consideration. However, the Bible tells us that when we come to our King in prayer, He already knows what we are going to ask for and He knows what we need better than we do. We have to remember that this One we're talking to is omniscient. He doesn't learn anything new. So if you're going to change His mind by your prayers, it won't be because you give Him new information.

Sometimes we change our minds because we realize that what we had intended to do was a bad plan, that we made a mistake in taking such a course. Perhaps we get counsel from someone who says, "Oh, R. C., you shouldn't do that because if you do, A, B, or C is going to follow, and it's going to mess everything up." Is this what happens with God when we come to Him in prayer? Can we come to Him and say: "God, what You're planning to do is not good. Let me counsel You to do the right thing"? That would be absurd. God never does anything that is not perfectly good, and we fallen human beings are certainly in no position to counsel Him.

In short, no prayer of any human being ever uttered in history ever changed the mind of God in the slightest, because His mind doesn't ever need to be changed. Sadly, when I say that to people, they react in horror. They say: "Why should we pray? What good is prayer if we can't change God's mind? Why should we even engage in this exercise? It's an exercise in futility." At that point, I have to remind them that, as I mentioned above, prayer *does* change things, all kinds of things. But the most important thing it changes is us. As we engage in this communion with God more deeply and come to know the One with whom we are speaking more intimately, that growing knowledge of God reveals to us all the more brilliantly who we are and our need to change in conformity to Him. Prayer changes us profoundly.

God did not give prayer to the church for His benefit. The Sovereign has condescended to give us an audience. He has invited us into the heavenly palace. He has lifted the scepter and told us to enter. We have access to His very throne. But sometimes we come into His presence far too casually. We come to Him and say, "Hi, God, how are you doing?" We talk to God with the kind of familiarity that breeds contempt. It's a familiarity that reveals we have forgotten who He is and who we are. We have forgotten that we are peasants in the presence of the King. Not just *a* king, but *the* King, the King of kings, the Lord of lords, the One who is absolutely sovereign.

I want you to notice that in the petitions of the Lord's Prayer, there is a word that recurs. The petitions speak of "Your name," "Your kingdom," and "Your will." The word *Your* keeps coming up in reference to things that are God's. Finally, in the fourth petition, we read, "Give us this day our daily bread." We have to go a long way into this prayer before we find any attention or concern given to us. The attention at the beginning of these petitions is on the exaltation of God and His concerns. In the initial phrases of the Lord's Prayer, Jesus fixes our gaze not on ourselves but on God.

People come to me and ask: "What are the rules for prayer? How should we approach God in prayer? What's the right way to pray?" I tell those who ask these kinds of questions that there are really only two rules that you have to keep in mind when you're in prayer, two things that should drive and govern and control your prayer life with the Almighty. You should remember who is being addressed and who is doing the speaking. That is, the first thing you are to remember in prayer is who it is you're talking to, because nothing will condition your prayer life more deeply than remembering that you're in conversation with God, the sovereign Creator and Ruler of the universe. Second, you are to remember who you are. You are not God. You are a creature. So prayer is not a conversation between peers; it is not a fireside chat among equals. This is the creature speaking to his sovereign Creator.

Finally, it is important to note Jesus' final words before beginning to spell out the Lord's Prayer itself. He did not say, "Pray *this*." Rather, He said, "In this manner, therefore, pray" (Matt. 6:9a). Jesus did not give His disciples a prayer they should slavishly repeat, though, as I noted above, repeating the prayer can be good and useful if it is handled correctly. Jesus' intent was to give His disciples a model prayer, an example to follow, one that would teach them transferable principles for conversation with God. Beginning in the next chapter, we will look closely at those principles.

TWO

Our Father in Heaven

If you have been involved in Christian groups that pray frequently or in church gatherings where individuals in the room take turns praying aloud, you may have noticed how common it is for Christians to begin their prayers with the word *Father*. The overwhelming majority of personal prayers begin with some form of reference to God as Father.

On the other hand, perhaps you haven't taken notice of the frequent use of the word *Father* in the prayers of believers. We have a tendency to take this title for God for granted. It is so familiar to us, so common to our life and to our liturgy, that we rarely give any thought to it. We fail to grasp what a radical thing it is to refer to God in this way.

The German theologian Joachim Jeremias, a New Testament scholar, did a study in which he searched through the Old

Testament writings and existent rabbinic writings from ancient Jewish sources. He could not find a single example ever of a Jewish writer or author addressing God directly as Father in prayer until the tenth century AD. He found examples of God being referred to as "the Father," but the word *Father* was never used in a direct form of personal address.

This is curious, because the Old Testament spoke about the nation of Israel as God's "son." Matthew's Gospel tells us that shortly after Jesus' birth in Bethlehem, an angel warned Joseph to take Mary and the baby to Egypt to escape the wrath of Herod. Matthew specifically notes that this event occurred as a fulfillment of an Old Testament prophecy, "Out of Egypt I called My Son" (Matt. 2:15b; Hosea 11:1). In its original context, this statement referred to the exodus, when Israel was delivered from its bondage in Egypt. On the night the Israelites were released from their captivity, God passed over the land, bringing the worst plague of all against Pharaoh and the Egyptians. He came to slay the firstborn son in every Egyptian household, including the household of Pharaoh. What was the significance of that? God was saying to the most powerful ruler on this planet, "Pharaoh, if you will not respect My son, I will kill your son." So there was a sense in which the Israelites were understood to be sons of God, which placed God in a fatherly role. However, the Israelites never addressed God as Father.

Jeremias also examined the prayers of Jesus, and there he made an equally fascinating discovery—in *every* prayer of Jesus recorded in the New Testament except one, He addresses God as Father. Jeremias says that the significance of this is that Jesus, who was a Jew and a rabbi, was making a departure from tradition.

It wasn't just a little departure; it was a radical departure. Of course, this departure aroused profound hostility from His contemporaries. When Jesus referred to God as His Father, His contemporaries—the Pharisees, for example—would become enraged. They understood that, in calling God His Father, He was making Himself equal with God (John 5:18). By addressing God in this familiar form, Jesus was indicating a profound sense of intimacy between Himself and God, showing that He was the unique Son of God.

One of the most important doctrines of the New Testament that gives expression to our redemption is the doctrine of adoption. By nature, the Bible says, we are children of wrath (Eph. 2:3). God is not our Father naturally, in terms of an intimate, personal, filial relationship. But we are adopted into the family of God in Christ. Christ is the *monogenes*, the only begotten Son of the Father. He is the only One who has the inherent right to address God as "Abba, Father" (Mark 14:36). But when He gave His disciples this model prayer, He invited them to use that personal form of address, which indicates an intensely familiar filial relationship. Of course, not only does the Son give us the right to address God as Father, but the Holy Spirit, as He assists us in our prayer lives, prompts us to cry, "Abba, Father!" (Gal. 4:6).

A Privilege of Adoption

With those facts as background, consider the way in which Jesus instructed His disciples to address God: "In this manner, therefore, pray: 'Our Father in heaven'" (Matt. 6:9a). Jesus was saying that not only was He allowed to address God as Father by virtue of His unique status as the Son of God, but even His followers had that privilege by virtue of their adoption.

This is not something to be taken lightly. Every time we say the Lord's Prayer, every time we open our mouths and say, "Our Father," we should be reminded of our adoption, that we have been grafted into Christ and have been placed in this intimate relationship with God, a relationship that we did not have by nature. It is a relationship that has been won for us by the perfect obedience of the Son, who received an inheritance that was promised to Him from the foundation of the world, which inheritance He shares with His brothers and sisters who are in Him.

In the nineteenth century, a new discipline was added to the curriculum of the study of religion. It was called "comparative religion." This was an attempt at understanding the great religions of the world not in isolation but, as the term itself suggests, in comparison with one another. This interest was brought about in part because of the shrinking of the globe as travel and communication became faster. In the past, it was common to find various religions clustered in certain geographical portions of the world and usually limited to ethnic groups or nationalities. But as the world became smaller and more interaction took place between the West and the East, Christians increasingly had to deal with Islam, Buddhism, Hinduism, Shintoism, Confucianism, and so on. The field of comparative religion was developed in an attempt to look at the various religions of this world and find common denominators.

It was during this period that the famous mountain analogy was developed. The idea was that God sits at the summit of a great mountain and that many roads go to the peak. Some of them go more or less directly from the base of the mountain to the top, while others bend and wind and twist and turn, taking a circuitous route to the summit. But the basic idea was that it doesn't really matter ultimately which road you take, because all of the roads lead to the top and eventually will bring you there. So if you're trying to get to God, you can go on the road of Christianity, Islam, Buddhism, or any of the others. All of these religions are just different roads, all going to the same place.

In German scholarship in the nineteenth century, particularly in this field of comparative religion, there was a German word that occurred over and over again in the titles of important books. It was the word *wesen*. This word can be translated in English as "being," "substance," or "essence." The frequent use of this word reflected the attempt in German scholarship to penetrate to the core beliefs of the various world religions, the fundamental substance, the essence of each of them. The sanguine conclusion of these scholars was that at the core of all world religions is the common affirmation of faith.

What Makes Christianity Christian?

One of those works was written by an outstanding German church historian, perhaps the most important church historian of the past two hundred years, Adolf von Harnack. He produced a work in German that subsequently was translated into English and became a best seller in the theological world. That book had a tremendous impact on theology at the end of the nineteenth century and into the twentieth century. The English edition was titled *What Is Christianity?* But the title in German was asking "What is the essence or being (*wesen*) of Christianity?" Harnack was asking what makes Christianity Christian.

Harnack came to the conclusion that the message of Christ and the core doctrines of biblical Christianity can be reduced to two fundamental propositions. You may never have heard of Harnack and you probably have never heard of *What Is Christianity?* but I'm sure you have heard these propositions. They are, first, the universal fatherhood of God, and second, the universal brotherhood of man.

You may think my next words are controversial or even shocking; you may be completely outraged, but hear me out. I think Harnack was wrong in his analysis of the essence of Christianity. I don't think these two propositions are at the core of the Christian faith. In fact, I don't think they're even a part of the Christian faith. I think these propositions are actually antithetical to the Christian faith. If you were to ask me to write a book titled *What Is Humanism?* or *What Is Nineteenth-Century Liberalism?* then I might say that those systems of thought can be reduced down to the universal fatherhood of God and the universal brotherhood of man. However, I can't agree that those propositions are of the essence of Christianity.

Why do I say this? I believe it is impossible to go to the Scriptures of the Old and New Testaments and find there the concept of the universal fatherhood of God. I can find a couple of passages that may support this concept only in a very tangential way. For example, when Paul is debating with the philosophers in Athens at Mars Hill, he makes the statement that "We are also His offspring" (Acts 17:28b). However, this is not a quotation from the Old Testament; it is a quotation from a pagan poet. It follows Paul's statement that we live and move and have our being in God, meaning we can speak of the universal fatherhood of God in the sense that He is the Creator of all people. We are all His offspring because He is the universal Begetter of the human race. However, when the Bible speaks of the fatherhood of God, it doesn't characteristically do so with regard simply to creation, but specifically to redemption. Since that is the case, the fatherhood of God is not inclusive, but exclusive and restricted.

So God is the Father of Jesus in a unique way—Christ is the "only begotten of the Father" (John 1:14). Then the fatherhood of God is extended to those who are adopted into His family by virtue of their union with Christ. Thus, far from teaching the *universal* fatherhood of God, the Bible teaches the *particular* fatherhood of God. Therefore, to call God "Father" in the New Testament sense of the word, in the sense of the word the way the church expresses it as the family of God, is to affirm the very uniqueness of Christianity. Yes, it's un-American and antihumanistic to question the universal fatherhood of God, but this idea is not a biblical concept.

Harnack's second proposition is deduced from the first. Since God is the Father of us all, we must all share a certain brotherhood or sisterhood. Again, however, this proposition cannot be deduced from the New Testament. I don't think the Bible teaches the universal brotherhood of men at all. You may respond: "Wait a minute. Doesn't the Bible teach us to love everyone? Shouldn't a brotherhood be a community where people love each other?" Yes, of course. But just because there is a community where people are obligated to love one another doesn't make that community a brotherhood or a sisterhood. Once again we need to see and understand the biblical categories. The brotherhood of which the New Testament speaks is the brotherhood or sisterhood of fellowship enjoyed by all those who are adopted into the family of God and who are in Christ. He is described as "the firstborn among many brethren" (Rom. 8:29b). I am in the brotherhood when I am linked to Christ by adoption. I am His adopted brother. Likewise, every other Christian who is in that special fellowship of the church participates in this special brotherhood. We are not born into it naturally; we must be reborn in order to be in this brotherhood. Therefore, when we speak about the universal brotherhood of man, we weaken or cheapen this crucial point that the New Testament makes about the singularity of the church as the company of the redeemed.

The Universal Neighborhood of Man

Why would anyone come to the conclusion that there is a universal brotherhood of man? I've already suggested one reason—they deduce it from the first of Harnack's two propositions, the universal fatherhood of God. But some come to this conclusion, as erroneous as it may be, because the Bible does indeed speak of something in terms of universality. It's not brotherhood but neighborhood. Not all men are my brothers, only those who are in Christ. However, all men are my neighbors, and I am required by God to treat these people as I would expect them to treat me. I am required to love my neighbor as much as I love myself. Jesus made it clear that the neighborhood is not restricted to the brotherhood. That was the mistake the Pharisees made. The Pharisees believed that all of the biblical obligations to love one's neighbor were limited to their fellow Jews, to the brotherhood. Based on that conclusion, they didn't have to be loving to Samaritans, for example.

In the parable of the good Samaritan, Jesus told the story of the man who went down to Jericho, but fell among thieves and was beaten, robbed, and left for dead. A Levite and a priest passed by and left the man suffering. However, a passing Samaritan took compassion on the man, stopped, anointed his wounds with oil, carried him to an inn, and paid the innkeeper for his ongoing care until such time as the Samaritan could come back and settle the bill. What was the occasion that prompted Jesus to tell this parable? He told that story in answer to a lawyer who asked, "Who is my neighbor?" (Luke 10:29). The story features a Samaritan and a Jew, two people who certainly did not consider themselves as part of a brotherhood. But Jesus was saying to that Jewish lawyer, "Even the Samaritan is your neighbor." Likewise, He is saying to us: "The Russian is your neighbor, the Asian is your neighbor, the pagan is your neighbor, the Buddhist is your neighbor, the Muslim is your neighbor. Every human being on the face of this earth is your neighbor, and you are to love that person as much as you love yourself." While it is not true that there is a universal brotherhood of man, it is quite biblical to say that there is a universal neighborhood. However, it requires only a slight shift to move from the idea of universal neighborhood to that of universal brotherhood.

I know people who struggle to address God as Father. People have said to me, "I can hardly bear to say it, because my earthly father was a cruel and insensitive person." People have told me of instances in which their fathers committed child abuse, and they have asked me: "After that experience, how could I possibly address God as Father? The word is repugnant to me." I can understand that reaction. I usually acknowledge that what makes the pain and torment they bear in their psyches so severe is the fact that these things didn't happen at the hands of a next-door neighbor, an uncle, or someone else—it was from the father. Nature itself teaches that they rightfully should expect much more from their earthly fathers than they have received.

When I talk to someone who is having difficulty using the word *Father* and wants to choke on it when he refers to God, I usually advise him that, as hard as it may be, to focus on the word that comes before it, *our*, because "our Father" is not his father. "Our Father" is not the father who violated him. It's our Father in heaven, our Father who has no abuse in Him, who will never violate anyone. We all need to learn to use this phrase and transfer to God the positive attributes that we so earnestly desire and so seriously miss in our earthly fathers.

When Jesus gave the Lord's Prayer, with its use of "Our Father" as the form of address, He gave us the unspeakable privilege of addressing God in the same terms of filial familiarity that Jesus Himself used. However, we must always remember that God is *our* Father. He is the Patriarch of the brotherhood.

He is the One who adopts the brothers and the sisters. As the brothers and the sisters are born of God and are reborn by the Spirit of God, they become the adopted children of God, which is a status and a privilege that is paramount to the New Testament concept of redemption. This status should be brought to the front of our minds every time we say the Lord's Prayer.

THREE

Hallowed Be Your Name

In my years of teaching seminary courses, I often played a game with my students. I said to them, "If you had the opportunity to write a new constitution for the United States of America, a constitution that would include a new bill of rights containing ten declarations, what would you choose for those foundational precepts?" I asked them whether they might want to include a law to safeguard the sanctity of human life or one to protect private property. Then I asked them whether they would consider using one of those ten declarations to mandate that parents be honored or to prohibit coveting. To top it all off, I asked whether any of them would vote for a foundational legal document that included in its top ten laws a mandate protecting the use of the name of God.

You see my point. When God gave such a document, constituted His people as a nation, and created the foundation for a godly society, He included in His top ten commandments a law that regulated the use of His name: "You shall not take the name of the LORD your God in vain" (Ex. 20:7a). The inclusion of this commandment in God's Old Testament law shows beyond doubt that He places a very high premium on the importance of His people recognizing His name as holy and treating it that way. We see that same premium in the prayer that Jesus gave to His disciples, the prayer we know as the Lord's Prayer.

As we've seen, the disciples came to Jesus with a request: "Lord, teach us to pray." In response, Jesus said, "In this manner . . . pray," which set the stage for His teaching of a model prayer, an example of the kind of conversation and communion believers should have with God. He then gave them authority to address God in prayer as "Our Father in heaven," and we looked at the significance of that form of address.

The next words of Jesus' model prayer are these: "Hallowed be Your name" (Matt. 6:9b). We have a tendency to read these words and to conclude that they are part of the address, that they are simply an acknowledgment of an existing truth. That is, we believe we are saying: "Our Father in heaven, Your name is holy." But that's not the format of the prayer. This line of the Lord's Prayer is not simply an assertion that God's name is holy. Rather, it's a petition.

Everyone knows what a petition is—it's a piece of paper that people pass around for others to sign in hopes that this written evidence of agreement on an issue will induce the government or the ruling body of some association to change the rules of the game. A petition, then, is a request. For this reason, those specific requests Jesus gave His disciples in the Lord's Prayer are known as the petitions. These are the priorities that Jesus indicated His disciples should ask for in their prayers. And the very first thing that Jesus told them to pray for was that the name of God would be regarded as holy.

What does it mean to say that God is holy? It means that He is different from anything that we experience or find in the material universe, that God the Creator differs from all creatures. The primary way in which God differs from all creatures is that He is uncreated and eternal, whereas each of us is created and finite. We are not eternal but temporal. If nothing else separates the Creator from the creature, it is that high, transcendent element of God's own being, so marvelous, so majestic that He is worthy of the adoration of every creature.

I can't emphasize too much how important it is that we grasp that this line of the Lord's Prayer is not just a part of the address but a petition. We must see this if we are to understand what Jesus is teaching us about prayer. Jesus is not saying, "Father, Your name is holy," but, "Father, may Your name be hallowed." That is, He is teaching us to ask that God's name would be regarded as sacred, that it would be treated with reverence, and that it would be seen as holy. We must see this if we are to pray according to the pattern Jesus set for us.

The Sacredness of God's Name

I find it striking that when Jesus taught the church how to pray, the first thing He chose to tell us to pray about is that the name of God might be regarded as sacred. Very few people today would list the hallowing of the name of God as a top priority for the supplications of the people of God. It almost seems foreign to our environment to place so much emphasis on proper treatment of a name.

Yet, I am aware that it annoys me when people simply mispronounce my name. I am embarrassed to think I am so vain and proud that it bothers me when people call me "Sprowl" or "Sproll" instead of "Sproul." When a person calls me "Sprowl," I'll say, "You call me Sprowl and I growl, my name is Sproul, it rhymes with soul. It's soul with 'pr.'" Do you feel similarly bothered when people mispronounce your name? I suspect you do. Why is that? It's because they don't seem to be taking you seriously. It suggests that they don't even have enough concern for you as a person to get your name right. We somehow feel slighted if our names are forgotten or mispronounced.

Well, God is not sensitive in the sense that He is upset or loses His dignity if someone doesn't regard Him properly with the pronunciation of His name. But Jesus gives this petition within the context of a set of petitions. The Lord's Prayer continues like this: "Hallowed be Your Name. Your kingdom come. Your will be done on earth as it is in heaven" (Matt. 6:9b–10). I'm going to take the liberty to speculate here. I often have wondered whether Jesus, when He set forth the priorities of prayer, had a reason for listing the petitions in the order that He did. First He listed "Hallowed be Your name," second was "Your kingdom come," and third was "Your will be done." Those petitions may be distinguished one from another, but they're so interconnected that we dare not divorce them from one another. I'm convinced that although we pray for the manifestation and the victory of the kingdom of God, it is futile to hope for the victory of God's kingdom on this planet until or unless the name of God is regarded as sacred, because God's kingdom does not come to people who have no respect for Him. Likewise, we pray that the will of God will be done in this world, but God's will is not done by people who do not regard Him with reverence and with adoration. So the very beginning of godliness, the very beginning of transformation in our lives and in our society, begins with our posture before the character of God.

The Importance of Our Words

I don't think that anything reveals the state of a person's soul more clearly than the words that come out of his mouth. I understand that Christians are capable of all kinds of sin, but I can't understand how a regenerate person could ever use the name of Jesus in a blasphemous way. How can you worship Someone whom you routinely blaspheme? I don't see how it's possible.

Before my conversion, I thought nothing of using the name of God or the name of Jesus in a blasphemous manner, as a mode of cursing. But after my conversion, I noticed an almost immediate change in my speech patterns. I couldn't find it within myself to blaspheme the names of God and Jesus anymore. Why not? Because I was in love. I had a profound affection for Christ and a profound sense of gratitude for God, and suddenly things that had rolled off my lips so easily prior to my conversion just simply would no longer come forth from my mouth. A second thing I noticed was that I had a kind of sensitivity to hearing that kind of language from my friends.

I realized that when my friends used the name of God or the name of Jesus in a blasphemous manner, they weren't thinking about what they were saying. I knew they didn't start out their day by saying, "Today I'm going to blaspheme God's name every time I open my mouth." It was simply a habit they had fallen into, an unconscious mode of expression, just as it had been in my life until that point. So even though the things my friends said bothered me, I could hardly feel judgmental toward them because I'd been just as guilty for speaking in this manner for years.

We have seen a radical change in the standards of what is permitted in terms of linguistic expression in our culture. We see evidence of the change in the movie theaters, where any form of expression is permissible now. There are still standards on broadcast television, certain words and phrases of a graphic nature that are not allowed, although there, too, the standards have been greatly relaxed. I can remember how, thirty years ago, it was not permissible to say the word *virgin* on national television because that word was considered too sexually suggestive. We've come a long way, haven't we?

However, I've noticed that even though some words and phrases are still forbidden on television, when it comes to the name of God, anything goes. We will not allow explicit erotic language on television, but we will allow blasphemy with regard to the name of God. I once watched a half-hour program and counted fifty-eight instances on that program when the name of God was treated with anything but reverence. This commonplace practice terrifies me, but most people today don't see it as a concern.

Several years ago, I read a magazine article about a truck driver who had been arrested in Maryland for drunk and disorderly conduct. He was verbally abusive to the arresting officers, so much so that by the time they got him to the magistrate for a hearing on this misdemeanor, they wanted the magistrate to throw the book at him. The magistrate saw that according to the statutes of the state of Maryland, the maximum penalty that he could impose on the truck driver for drunk and disorderly conduct was a fine of $100 and thirty days in jail. However, he also noticed on the law books a prohibition against public blasphemy. So he assigned another thirty days in jail and another $100 fine because, in his verbal abuse of the officers during the time of his arrest, the truck driver had blasphemed the name of God. The magazine in which I read about this incident published an editorial vehemently protesting this outdated, arcane, puritanical law that was still on the books and was still being enforced in our modern and sophisticated culture. The editors were furious that anyone in America in this day and age would be penalized by the law for publicly blaspheming God. I couldn't help but think that the truck driver should be glad he didn't live in ancient Israel, because if he had blasphemed the name of God in that culture, it would have cost him not merely thirty days in jail and $100, but his life. We live in a topsy-turvy world, where the values are radically different than the values of the biblical worldview.

If God in the Ten Commandments saw the need to require reverence for His name in the time of the exodus, and if Jesus saw the need to call on His disciples to pray that God's name would be regarded as holy in the Jewish culture of two thousand years ago, how much more crucial is it that we pray that the name of God would be hallowed in our own time? This petition, "Hallowed be Your name," should be on our lips every day, indeed every time we hear the name of God or Jesus casually blasphemed.

The Foundational Petition

By placing this as the first petition of the Lord's Prayer, Jesus was giving it a place of priority. He was saying that a proper attitude toward God's name is the basis of everything, because how we live before God is determined by our attitude toward Him and our view of who He is. No worship, no adoration, and no obedience can flow from a heart that has no regard for the name of God. There's a psychological truism here. How is it possible for someone to have a high regard for God, an authentic reverence for God, a genuine fear of God, and at the same time have a frivolous attitude toward the use of the name of God? Jesus says here that the way in which we regard the name of God reveals the state of our hearts with respect to our attitude toward God Himself. A lack of regard for His name reveals more clearly than anything else a lack of regard for Him. So when Jesus says we should pray that God's name be regarded as holy, He is saying that we should regard Him as holy, and that such a posture of reverence, awe, and respect for God should define everything in our lives.

Before God's kingdom can come to earth the way it has already come to heaven, and before His will can be done on earth the way it is done right now in heaven, the name of God has to be hallowed. There is no blasphemy in heaven. There is nothing profane in heaven. No one in heaven, seraphim, cherubim, or the spirits of men who have departed to join the assembly on high, ever does anything but the will of God in heaven, and they do it joyously, happily, for His glory. If we would honor Him here on earth, we must begin by regarding His name as holy and treating it that way.

FOUR

Your Kingdom Come

Recently, my wife and I became engrossed in a television broadcast of the annual opening of Parliament in London. We watched in rapt attention as the TV cameras focused on Queen Elizabeth and Prince Philip leaving Buckingham Palace to go to the Houses of Parliament in a beautifully ornate coach drawn by magnificent horses. They had all of the pageantry of England—the Beefeaters in their full regalia, liveried footmen, and so forth. Meanwhile, London's Bobbies cleared the traffic and made the path ready for the appearance of the queen. Later there were panoramic shots from inside the Houses of Parliament, and we saw the lords dressed in their formal garb and wearing their ceremonial white wigs.

It was striking to witness this spectacle at the beginning of the twenty-first century, in our modern sophisticated society.

Here were people by the hundreds dressed in clothing that looked like it belonged in the Middle Ages and going through rituals that seem thoroughly outdated. I couldn't help but wonder, as I watched, what it is about human nature that likes to create ceremony of this sort. Why do we like to use aesthetic devices to draw attention to the importance of certain events? And more to the point, I also wondered why Americans such as my wife and I can become so preoccupied with the doings of the British royal family. Indeed, why do we take such delight in kings and queens, princes and princesses, whether in real life or in fairy tales such as we read to our children? After all, we're citizens of a nation that rejected monarchy.

When my friend John Guest, who was a noted evangelist in England, first came to the United States in the late 1960s, his first exposure to American culture was in the city of Philadelphia. During his first couple of days there, his hosts escorted him around the city to attractions such as Independence Hall and the Liberty Bell, and they told him stories of the American Revolution to introduce him to the history of this new world he was embracing as his home. John was enjoying all of this until they went to Germantown, just outside Philadelphia, and visited an antiques store that specialized in Americana. Among the items in this shop were placards and signs that displayed some of the battle cries and slogans of the Revolutionary era, such as, "No Taxation without Representation" and "Don't Tread on Me." But the placard that drew his keenest attention was one that announced with bold letters, "We Serve No Sovereign Here." John told me later: "That sign stopped me in my tracks. I had left my native land and come across the Atlantic Ocean in response to a call, a vocation to be a minister of the gospel, to proclaim the kingdom of God. But on seeing this sign, I was filled with fear and consternation. I thought, 'How can I possibly preach the kingdom of God to people who have a profound aversion to sovereignty?'"

I would suggest that despite our bold assertions that we serve no sovereign, our delight in the pageantry of royalty reveals a certain nostalgia, perhaps a deep longing for the restoration of monarchy. After all, we impose a kind of royalty on our leaders. The days of the Kennedy administration are remembered as the "Camelot" era. We speak of certain jazz musicians as "the Count" or "the Duke," and we remember Elvis Presley as "the King." As I noted above, we like to watch the pageantry of royalty and to read stories about princes and princesses. Could it be we retain an interest in royalty because we recognize that in this freedom we enjoy, something is missing? Perhaps what is missing is that which we need most desperately—an awakening to authentic sovereignty.

In the Lord's Prayer, we see the priorities of prayer that Jesus gave for His church. The first petition He gave is "Hallowed be Your name." As we saw in the previous chapter, this petition teaches us that we are to regard God's name as holy and to pray that our blasphemous culture would do the same. Praying this petition places us in a posture of veneration—we see God as the One who is altogether holy. That understanding, in turn, moves us into a posture of obeisance. Always in Scripture, when someone recognizes that awesome holiness of God, he falls on his face before Him. Likewise, we are to bow before God just as a subject kneels before his king. So we see that there is a continuity in these petitions of the Lord's Prayer. Jesus says first of all, "Hallowed be Your Name." Then the very next petition is "Your kingdom come." He moves immediately from a petition about the veneration of the name of God to one about the manifestation of the kingdom of God.

If there is any motif that ties together the Old Testament and the New Testament, it is the theme of the kingdom of God. Even though the New Testament opens with the announcement that the kingdom of God is coming, that something new is about to take place in the unfolding history of redemption, there is still continuity with the past. In one sense, the kingdom of God has always been present, having been established in the Garden of Eden. God didn't have to wait until the New Testament to be crowned as the Sovereign Ruler over the universe—He was King over Adam and Eve. Later, when God created the nation of Israel at Mount Sinai, He delivered His law to them as the King of heaven and earth. He separated the Israelites to Himself and told them: "I am the Lord your God . . . You shall have no other gods before Me" (Ex. 20:2–3).

Rejecting God as King

There came a point in Israel's history when the people were not satisfied to have God as their King. In the book of 1 Samuel we read: "Then all the elders of Israel gathered together and came to Samuel at Ramah, and said to him, 'Look, you are old, and your sons do not walk in your ways. Now make us a king to judge us like all the nations'" (8:4–5). The people wanted to have a human king so they would be like all the other people groups. God had declared that He was Israel's King, but now the people wanted an earthly king.

The text of this narrative tells us that Samuel was displeased by this request, so he took his concerns to God. God said to him, "Heed the voice of the people in all that they say to you; for they have not rejected you, but they have rejected Me; that I should not reign over them" (1 Sam. 8:7). Isn't that interesting? God said: "Samuel, you're bent out of shape because they're coming to you and they're saying, 'You're old and your sons don't walk in the way you've walked, so we don't want to have to follow them. Instead, we want a king.'" Samuel apparently felt that in making this demand for a king, the people were rejecting him and his ministry. But that wasn't how God saw it; He declared that the people were rejecting Him and His kingship. In their arrogance, the people of Israel were saying of God, "He shall not reign over us."

When God told Samuel to grant the people their request for a king, He also said, "Solemnly forewarn them, and show them the behavior of the king who will reign over them" (1 Sam. 8:9b). So Samuel said to the people:

> "This will be the behavior of the king who will reign over you: He will take your sons and appoint them for his own chariots and to be his horsemen, and some will run before his chariots. He will appoint captains over his thousands and captains over his fifties, will set some to plow his ground and reap his harvest, and some to make his weapons of war and equipment for his chariots. He will take your daughters to be perfumers, cooks, and bakers. And he will take the best of your fields, your

vineyards, and your olive groves, and give them to his servants. He will take a tenth of your grain and your vintage, and give it to his officers and servants. And he will take your male servants, your female servants, your finest young men, and your donkeys, and put them to his work. He will take a tenth of your sheep. And you will be his servants. And you will cry out on that day because of your king whom you have chosen for yourselves, and the LORD will not hear you in that day." (1 Sam. 8:11–18)

This is a litany of bad news. Samuel warned the people that the king would conscript the people's sons and daughters for his army and his staff. He would tax them at a rate of ten percent. He would make the people themselves his servants. Samuel warned the people that they would not like this, but God would not hear their cries for relief. Nevertheless, the people said, "No, but we will have a king over us" (v. 19b).

Did you catch the word that appears most frequently in this warning from Samuel? It is the word *take*. The king, Samuel says, will take, take, and take some more. Yet Scripture speaks of God as a King who gives and gives, blessing His people with every good and perfect gift. However, we don't want a King who will give. The madness of human folly is that we want a king who will take just so we can be like everyone else. In our fallenness, it seems that anything is better than to live in the kingdom of God, where God is the King.

You remember how the story unfolded. Saul was selected as Israel's first king, and in the early days of his monarchy, he reigned well. He pledged to be submissive to the law of God. Sadly, his power corrupted him and drove him to madness, so that God had to remove him from the throne and replace him with David. David, of course, was the greatest king of Israel, but even he did not always rule wisely and well. Much the same was true for David's son, Solomon. Then, after Solomon died and his son Rehoboam came to the throne, in a very short period of time the kingdom was divided. And the history of the kings of the north and the south from that day forward reads like a rogue's gallery of corruption, all of which God foretold through Samuel.

Rejecting Christ as King

The feelings of antipathy against the reign of God run so deep in the human heart that Jesus was brought before the Roman authorities on the grounds that He was making Himself King. He didn't make Himself King, the Father made Him King. But just as God had been rejected as King by the ancient Israelites, Jesus was rejected as King in the time of His incarnation. The Jewish leaders brought Him before Pilate, the Roman governor. That led to a fascinating exchange:

> Pilate . . . said to Him, "Are You the King of the Jews?"
> . . . Jesus answered, "My kingdom is not of this world. If My kingdom were of this world, My servants would fight, so that I should not be delivered to the Jews; but now My kingdom is not from here." Pilate therefore said to Him, "Are You a king then?" Jesus answered, "You say rightly that I am a king. For this cause I was

born, and for this cause I have come into the world, that
I should bear witness to the truth." (John 18:33b–37a)

What was the truth to which this King, whose kingdom
is not of this world, was bearing witness? It was the kingdom
of God. He was testifying to the reign of the true King. Thus,
when Jesus told His followers to pray, "Your kingdom come,"
He was making them participants in His own mission to spread
the reign of God on this planet so that it might reflect the way
God's reign is established in heaven to this day.

I had been a Christian only a few months when I was
invited to a Christmas party hosted by my pastor and his wife at
their home. This minister was an unreconstructed, nineteenth-
century liberal theologian who did not believe in the miracles
of Jesus or in the resurrection of Christ, so he was somewhat
annoyed at my newfound zeal for biblical Christianity. During
this party, he called me aside and asked me this question: "R.
C., what is the kingdom of God?" I had no earthly idea. I didn't
know what he was asking and I certainly had no idea why he
was asking it.

Well, suppose someone asked you that question: What
is the kingdom of God? How would you respond? The easy
answer would be to note that a kingdom is that territory over
which a king reigns. Since we understand that God is the Creator of all things, the extent of His realm must be the whole
world. Manifestly, then, the kingdom of God is wherever God
reigns, and since He reigns everywhere, the kingdom of God is
everywhere.

But I think my pastor was getting at something else. Certainly the New Testament gets at something else. We see this when John the Baptist comes out of the wilderness with his urgent announcement, "Repent, for the kingdom of God is at hand." We see it again when Jesus appears on the scene with the same pronouncement. If the kingdom of God consists of all of the universe over which God reigns, why would anyone announce that the kingdom of God was *near* or *about to come to pass*. Obviously, John the Baptist and Jesus meant something more about this concept of the kingdom of God.

The Kingdom of the Messiah

At the heart of this theme is the idea of God's messianic kingdom. It is a kingdom that will be ruled by God's appointed Messiah, who will be not just the Redeemer of His people, but their King. So when John speaks of the radical nearness of this breakthrough, the intrusion of the kingdom of God, he's speaking of this kingdom of the Messiah.

At the end of Jesus' life, just as He was about to depart from this earth, His disciples had the opportunity to ask Him one last question. They asked, "Lord, will You at this time restore the kingdom to Israel?" (Acts 1:6b). I can easily imagine that Jesus might have been somewhat frustrated by this question. I would have expected Him to say, "How many times do I have to tell you, I'm *not* going to restore the kingdom to Israel?" But that's not what He said; He gave a patient and gentle answer. He said: "It is not for you to know times or seasons which the Father has put in His own authority. . . . But you shall receive power when the Holy Spirit has come upon you; and you shall be witnesses to Me in Jerusalem, and in all Judea and Samaria, and to the end of the earth" (Acts 1:7–8). What did He mean? What was He getting at?

When Jesus told Pilate, "My kingdom is not of this world," was He indicating that His kingdom was something spiritual that takes place in our hearts or was He speaking of something else? The whole Old Testament called attention not to a kingdom that would simply appear in people's hearts, but to a kingdom that would break through into this world, a kingdom that would be ruled by God's anointed Messiah. For this reason, during His earthly ministry, Jesus made comments such as, "If I cast out demons with the finger of God, surely the kingdom of God has come upon you" (Luke 11:20). Similarly, when Jesus sent out seventy disciples on a preaching mission, He instructed them to tell impenitent cities that "The kingdom of God has come near you" (Luke 10:11b). How could the kingdom be *upon* the people or *near* them? The kingdom of God was near to them because the King of the kingdom was there. When He came, Jesus inaugurated God's kingdom. He didn't consummate it, but He started it. And when He ascended into heaven, He went there for His coronation, for His investiture as the King of kings and Lord of lords.

So Jesus' kingship is not something that remains in the future. Christ is King right this minute. He is in the seat of the highest cosmic authority. All authority in heaven and on earth has been given to God's anointed Son (Matt. 28:18).

In 1990, I was invited into Eastern Europe to do a series of lectures in three countries, first in Czechoslovakia, then in Hungary, and finally in Romania. As we were leaving Hungary, we were warned that the border guards in Romania were quite hostile to Americans and that we should be prepared to be hassled and possibly even arrested at the border.

Sure enough, when our rickety train reached the border of Romania, two guards got on. They couldn't speak English, but they pointed for our passports, then pointed to our luggage. They wanted us to bring our bags down from the luggage rack and open them up, and they were very brusque and rude. Then, suddenly, their boss appeared, a burly officer who spoke some broken English. He noticed that one of the women in our group had a paper bag in her lap, and there was something peeking out of it. The officer said: "What this? What in bag?" Then he opened the bag and pulled out a Bible. I thought, "Uh-oh, now we're in trouble." The officer began leafing through the Bible, looking over the pages very rapidly. Then he stopped and looked at me. I was holding my American passport, and he said, "You no American." And he looked at Vesta and said, "You no American." He said the same thing to the others in our group. But then he smiled and said, "I am not Romanian." By now we were quite confused, but he pointed at the text, gave it to me, and said, "Read what it says." I looked at it and it said, "Our citizenship is in heaven" (Phil. 3:20a). The guard was a Christian. He turned to his subordinates and said: "Let these people alone. They're OK. They're Christians." As you can imagine, I said, "Thank you, Lord." This man understood something about the kingdom of God—that our first place of citizenship is in the kingdom of God.

I had a crisis on this point in my last year of seminary, when I was a student pastor of a Hungarian refugee church in Western Pennsylvania. It was a little group of about one hundred people, many of whom didn't speak English. Someone donated an American flag to the church, which I placed in the chancel, across from the Christian flag. My crisis came the next week, when one of the elders, who was a veteran, came to me and said, "Reverend, you've got it all wrong there on the chancel." I asked, "What's the matter?" He said: "Well, the law of our land requires that any time any flag is displayed with the American flag, it must be placed in a subordinate position to the American flag. The way you have it arranged here, the American flag is subordinate to the Christian flag. That has to change." Anyone who has lived outside this country knows how wonderful this place is. I love it and I honor it, along with its symbols, including the flag. But as I listened to this elder speak, I asked myself, how can the Christian flag be subordinate to any national flag? The kingdom of God trumps every earthly kingdom. I'm a Christian first, an American second. I owe allegiance to the American flag, but I have a higher allegiance to Christ, because He is my King. So I had a dilemma. I didn't want to violate the law of the United States and I didn't want to communicate that the kingdom of God is subordinate to a human government. So I solved the dilemma easily enough—I took both flags out of the church.

We experience this conflict of kingdoms when Jesus tells us to pray, "Your kingdom come." What does this mean? What are we praying for when we speak this petition? As we've noted in previous chapters, there is a logic that runs like a ribbon through the Lord's Prayer. Each of the petitions is connected to the others. The first petition Jesus taught us was, "Hallowed be Your name," which is a plea that the name of God would be regarded as holy. Manifestly, unless and until the name of God is regarded as holy, His kingdom will not and cannot come to this world. But we who *do* regard His name as holy then have the responsibility to make the kingdom of God manifest.

John Calvin said it is the task of the church to make the invisible kingdom visible. We do that by living in such a way that we bear witness to the reality of the kingship of Christ in our jobs, our families, our schools, and even our checkbooks, because God in Christ is King over every one of these spheres of life. The only way the kingdom of God is going to be manifest in this world before Christ comes is if we manifest it by the way we live as citizens of heaven and subjects of the King.

FIVE

Your Will Be Done

Over the years of my ministry, I've been asked many questions about the Bible, about theology, and about Christian living. But the question I probably have been asked more than any other is this one: how can I know the will of God for my life? If there's any concept about which there's confusion among believers today, it is the will of God.

This issue crops up in the Lord's Prayer, the model prayer Jesus gave to His disciples in response to their request that He teach them how to pray. We've seen that He taught them to pray, first, "Hallowed be Your name," asking that the name of God would be regarded as holy. Then He enjoined them to pray, "Your kingdom come," which is a request that Christ's rule and reign would be made manifest in the world. The third petition of the Lord's Prayer is closely related to the first two and flows out of them in a sense. This petition is, "Your will be done on earth as it is in heaven" (Matt. 6:10b).

At first glance, it seems incredible that Jesus told His followers to pray that the will of God would be done on earth as it is in heaven. In fact, it seems almost heretical that Jesus would give His church such a mandate. Didn't He know that the will of God is *always* accomplished? Didn't He understand the biblical teaching on divine sovereignty, the truth that all things come to pass because God has decreed that they should?

When I'm asked about the will of God and I try to unravel this difficult subject, I usually start by reminding people that there are at least two different Greek words in the New Testament that are translated by the English word "will." These words, *thelema* and *boulema*, have several nuances of meaning, so it's not always immediately apparent by looking at a passage from the New Testament exactly what is meant by the will of God. However, there are three ways in which this concept is most commonly understood.

The first is what we call the sovereign, efficacious will of God. When the Bible speaks of the will of God in this sense, it is describing the will that causes whatever He decrees to come to pass. When God willed the universe to be created and said, "Let there be light," that expression of His sovereign will was instantly fulfilled; as Genesis says, "there was light." God spoke and the lights came on. Likewise, when Christ commanded Lazarus to rise from the dead and come out of his tomb, that command was efficacious—Lazarus obeyed instantly and immediately.

The sovereign, efficacious will of God is the will that brings to pass whatsoever He decrees.

Second, the Bible speaks of the will of God with respect to what we call His preceptive will. The preceptive will has to do with His law and commandments, the precepts He issues to regulate the behavior of His creation. It is the will of God that you have no other gods before Him, that you honor your father and your mother, that you remember the Sabbath Day, and so forth. Please note that the preceptive will of God can be violated and is violated every day. Being sinners, we disobey the will of God.

Third, the Bible speaks of the will of God in terms of His basic disposition or inclination. In this sense, God's will has to do with what is pleasing or displeasing to Him.

Let me illustrate how a verse of Scripture can be interpreted differently if we apply these different nuances of meaning. The Bible says, "The Lord is . . . not *willing* that any should perish but that all should come to repentance" (2 Peter 3:9, emphasis added). If the text means that God does not will that any should perish in the sovereign, efficacious sense, then it must be the case that none perish. If it means that He does not will that any should perish in the preceptive sense, it simply means that God has stated that no one is to engage in the activity of perishing, and to do so is a sin. If it is referring to God's disposition, it is simply saying that He is not pleased when someone perishes, that He does not enjoy the reality that not all are saved. Obviously, the first two understandings can be ruled out by teachings found elsewhere in Scripture, so that we may conclude that Peter is telling us that God takes no pleasure in the death of the wicked.

Jesus' Intended Meaning

Clearly this concept of the will of God is central to our under-standing of the Christian life and of the Scriptures. And we see that it is important even in our prayer life, for Jesus instructs us to pray that God's will would be done. But what precisely was Jesus telling His disciples to pray for when He gave them this petition?

This petition *could be* a plea that God's sovereign will might be accomplished. If ever there was a prayer request that we could know for certain would come to pass, it would be that one, for we know that the will of God is going to be done ultimately. If this is the correct understanding, then Jesus is saying, "I want you to remember again, when you're on your knees before God, who He is and who you are, and whose will is going to prevail." We certainly need frequent reminders of that truth. If I had a dollar for every professing Christian who has told me that the sovereignty of God is limited by the free will of man, I'd be very wealthy. I can only hope that those who make that statement haven't really thought about it very deeply, because it comes per-ilously close to blasphemy in that it makes man sovereign. The better approach is to say, "Yes, we have free will, but our free will is always and everywhere limited by God's sovereignty." When there's a conflict between my will and God's will, mine has to give way. Not my will, but His will, is sovereign. So perhaps Jesus is simply giving us a reminder here of who is sovereign, building into the Lord's Prayer a safeguard against an exalted view of the human will and providing a way for His people to acknowledge God's sovereignty.

However, I don't think that's the point. I say that because Jesus does not simply tell us to pray "Your will be done." Instead, He adds a qualifier, telling us to pray that God's will might be done "on earth as it is in heaven." These words suggest that there is a discrepancy between the accomplishment of whatever will of God Jesus has in view here on earth and its accomplishment in heaven.

We know that the sovereign will of God is always accomplished, not just in heaven but also on earth. That's why I do not think Jesus is referring here to the sovereign will of God. I think He must have the preceptive will of God in view, because the preceptive will of God is always obeyed by angels and by glorified believers in heaven. There is no sin in heaven. There is no conflict between the will of the creatures who are gathered around the presence of God and His holy will. This is because all who are in heaven have been brought into full conformity to the law of God. Rather than chafing against God's law, they glory in it.

In its very first question, the Westminster Shorter Catechism asks, "What is the chief end of man?" It then answers, "Man's chief end is to glorify God, and to enjoy him for ever." When I learned that question and answer as a child, it didn't make sense to me, although I got the message. I concluded that in order to glorify God, I had to obey Him; that I had to do what God wanted me to do rather than what I wanted to do. In short, I understood that I was supposed to be a good boy, but I couldn't see how there could be any enjoyment in that. Even after years of studying theology, I still struggle with it. You struggle with it too. Because we are fallen beings, we believe we will find joy and pleasure not in obedience to God but in sin. That prospect of joy and pleasure is what makes sin so attractive. However, there's a difference between joy and pleasure, an eternal difference. In that first question, the catechism is seeking to communicate the link between the glorification of God and joy. Our chief end, our main purpose in our existence, our primary reason for being, is to glorify God. There's a bonus in that: as we glorify Him through obedience, we enjoy Him.

Those who are gathered around the presence of God in heaven are doing two things. First, they're glorifying God. Isn't it interesting that the final stage of our sanctification is described in the New Testament as "glorification"? We will be glorified, and our glorification will be unto His glorification. The glorified ones are the ones who glorify God in heaven. Second, the believers now in heaven are enjoying God. The glorification of God in heaven brings unspeakable, eternal, uninterrupted joy. Jesus told His disciples that He had come so that "your joy may be full" (John 15:11b), and that fullness occurs when we reach heaven.

In this petition, then, Jesus is affirming that the will of God is done in heaven. However, He is also affirming that it is not done here. People here on earth do not strive to glorify God. They do not seek the kingdom of God. They do not hallow the name of God. So Jesus says we ought to pray, "Your will be done on earth as it is in heaven."

"If It Be Your Will . . ."

To my great distress, I sometimes hear people say, in their zeal for fervency and efficacy in prayer, that we should never qualify our prayer requests with the words "if it be Your will." Some will even say that to attach those words, those conditional terms, to our prayers is an act of unbelief. We are told today that in the boldness of faith we are to "name it and claim it." I suppose I should be more measured in my response to this trend, but I can't think of anything more foreign to the teaching of Christ. We come to the presence of God in boldness, but never in arrogance. Yes, we can name and claim those things God has clearly promised in Scripture. For instance, we can claim the certainty of forgiveness if we confess our sins before Him, because He promises that. But when it comes to getting a raise, purchasing a home, or finding healing from a disease, God hasn't made those kind of specific promises anywhere in Scripture, so we are not free to name and claim those things.

As I mentioned earlier, when we come before God, we must remember two simple facts—who He is and who we are. We must remember that we're talking to the King, the Sovereign One, the Creator, but we are only creatures. If we will keep those facts in mind, we will pray politely. We will say, "By Your leave," "As You wish," "If You please," and so on. That's the way we go before God. To say that it is a manifestation of unbelief or a weakness of faith to say to God "if it be Your will" is to slander the very Lord of the Lord's Prayer.

It was Jesus, after all, who, in His moment of greatest passion, prayed regarding the will of God. In his Gospel, Luke tells us that immediately following the Last Supper:

> Coming out, He went to the Mount of Olives, as He was accustomed, and His disciples also followed Him. When He came to the place, He said to them, "Pray that you may not enter into temptation." And He was

withdrawn from them about a stone's throw, and He knelt down and prayed, saying, "Father, if it is Your will, take this cup away from Me; nevertheless not My will, but Yours, be done." Then an angel appeared to Him from heaven, strengthening Him. And being in agony, He prayed more earnestly. Then His sweat became like great drops of blood falling down to the ground. (Luke 22:39–44)

It is important to see what Jesus prays here. He says, "Not My will, but Yours, be done." Jesus was not saying, "I don't want to be obedient" or "I refuse to submit." Jesus was saying: "Father, if there's any other way, all things being equal, I would rather not have to do it this way. What You have set before Me is more ghastly than I can contemplate. I'm entering into My grand passion and I'm terrified, but if this is what You want, this is what I'll do. Not My will, but Your will, be done, because My will is to do Your will."

I also want you to notice what happened after Jesus prayed. Luke tells us that an angel came to Him and strengthened Him. The angel was the messenger of God. He came from heaven with the Father's answer to Jesus' prayer. That answer was this: "You must drink the cup."

This is what it means to pray that the will of God would be done. It is the highest expression of faith to submit to the sovereignty of God. The real prayer of faith is the prayer that trusts God no matter whether the answer is yes or no. It takes no faith to "claim," like a robber, something that is not ours to claim. We are to come to God and tell Him what we want, but we must trust Him to give the answer that is best for us. That is what Jesus did.

Because Luke tells us that the Father sent an angel to strengthen His Son, I would expect Jesus' agony of soul to have been alleviated. It appears, however, that with the coming of the strength from the angel came an increase in the agony of Christ, an increase so profound that He began to sweat so profusely that it was "like great drops of blood." In a sermon on Luke 22:44, Jonathan Edwards said that this increase in Jesus' agony was due to a full realization of the will of God for Him in His passion. He had come to the garden with the fear that He would have to drink the cup. Once He knew it was indeed God's will that He drink it, He had a new fear—that He would not be able to do it. In other words, Jesus now was in agony that He not come short of complete and perfect obedience to the will of God.

But He did it. He drank the cup to the last drop. And in that moment, Jesus didn't give us words to show us how to pray; He gave us His life as an example of praying that the will of God would be done on earth as it is in heaven.

SIX

Give Us This Day Our Daily Bread

Christians often use a simple acrostic as a guide to prayer: A-C-T-S. Each of the letters in this acrostic stands for one of the key elements of prayer:

Adoration
Confession
Thanksgiving
Supplication

But not only does this acrostic remind us of the elements of prayer, it shows us the priority we ought to give to each. The first element of prayer should be adoration, or praise. The Psalms, which are inspired samples of godly prayer, are heavily weighted on the side of adoration. I've noticed over many years that as we grow in the discipline and in the delight of prayer, it seems that we naturally spend more and more of our time on this first element. Second, prayer should include confession of our sin; as we remember who we are when we come into God's presence, we see that we have come short of His holiness and have need of His forgiveness. Third, when we pray, we should always give thanks, remembering the grace and mercy God has shown toward us. Fourth, prayer rightly includes supplication or petition, bringing our requests for the needs of others and ourselves to God.

I think this is a helpful acrostic for remembering both the elements and the priorities of prayer. Unfortunately, we often spell our prayer life something like S-C-A-T, because we start with supplication and spend very little time, if any, on adoration, confession, and thanksgiving.

When we look at the Lord's Prayer, we see adoration at least implied in the petition "Hallowed be Your name." Jesus acknowledged that God's name is holy. We certainly see confession in the petition "Forgive us our debts," which we will examine in the next chapter. And there are supplications. However, it seems that the T is conspicuously absent. Where in the Lord's Prayer do we find any overt expression of gratitude to God? It's not there. That's strange, for as the apostle Paul taught, thanksgiving should always be included in our prayers: "Be anxious for nothing, but in everything by prayer and supplication, *with thanksgiving*, let your requests be made known to God" (Phil. 4:6, emphasis added).

Even though thanksgiving is not explicitly mentioned in the Lord's Prayer, I think it is implied in the petition that is our focus for this chapter: "Give us this day our daily bread" (Matt.

6:11). My reason for making this assertion is simple: we are to be alert not only to the need that we have daily for food, but to the reality of God's daily provision for our needs. That realization, of course, should induce us to an attitude of thanksgiving.

In previous chapters, we have noted that the Lord's Prayer begins with the address, "Our Father in heaven," and then moves through the petitions, beginning with "Hallowed be Your name." The focus of the prayer in its initial petitions is on God's glory and His kingdom. That's where the focus of our prayers needs to be. But then a shift occurs. With the fourth petition, Jesus begins to show His disciples how they ought to pray for their own needs. It is in this petition that we ask the Father to provide our daily bread.

The God Who Gives

This simple request has much to teach us, and I want us to note each element of it. First, notice that Jesus didn't teach us to pray that God would sell us our daily bread or render it to us in exchange for our service; instead, in this petition, we manifestly ask God to *give* us something. We ask Him to give us daily bread. We are so needy as to be destitute, but He owns "the cattle on a thousand hills" (Ps. 50:10b), so we go to Him as beggars asking for His charity. Scripture assures us that we can depend on Him to respond to such requests, for He is a giving God: "Every good and every perfect gift is from above, and comes down from the Father of lights" (James 1:17a).

God gives His gifts in order to provide for the needs of His people, for He is a God of providence. In the book of Genesis,

Moses tells us of God's great promise to Abraham that he would be the father of a great nation, that his descendants would be as the grains of sand on the seashore and as the stars in the sky. At the time the promise was made, Abraham's wife, Sarah, was barren. Finally, after many years elapsed, Sarah brought forth a son, whose name was Isaac. There was no happier set of parents in all of history than those two on the day God began to fulfill His promise in their old age. Just a few years later, however, there came a day when God said to Abraham, "Take now your son, your only son Isaac, whom you love, and go to the land of Moriah, and offer him there as a burnt offering on one of the mountains of which I shall tell you" (Gen. 22:2). God was saying, "I gave you this gift, Isaac, but now I want you to give him back to Me."

To his credit, Abraham did not hesitate. We're told that he "rose early in the morning" and set out on the three-day journey to Moriah. But when he and Isaac came to God's appointed mountain, and they were climbing up toward the conclusion of this heart-wrenching episode, Isaac noticed that one of the key requirements for a sacrifice seemed to be missing. So he said to Abraham, "Look, the fire and the wood, but where is the lamb for a burnt offering?" (v. 7b). Abraham didn't say, "You are the sacrifice." Instead, he took a deep breath and said to his son, "My son, God will provide for Himself the lamb for a burnt offering" (v. 8). He was trusting God to provide a sacrifice other than Isaac, and God proved faithful to do just that, staying Abraham's hand in the moment when he was about to sacrifice Isaac and providing a ram instead (vv. 12–13).

This is the first occasion in the Bible when the idea of divine providence is mentioned. Providence is about God's provision.

An integral element of that providence is His provision for our ultimate need of salvation—He provided Jesus, the Lamb without blemish, who was crucified for us. The God of providence is also concerned about our mundane, everyday needs, such as food to eat, water to drink, clothes to wear, and shelter for our bodies. Therefore, in His providence, He makes the crops grow, He makes the rains fall, and He provides what we need for clothing and homes. He gives us what we need for daily life.

David wrote, "I have been young, and now am old; yet I have not seen the righteous forsaken, nor his descendants begging bread" (Ps. 37:25). That's a tremendous testimony to the constancy with which God answers the prayers of His people when they bring their needs to Him.

Therefore, in this petition we are praying: "In Your sovereign providence, O God, please give us what we need. As You care for us, please provide us with the things we require for life in this world."

Just in passing, I think it is important to note that there is a synergistic relationship between divine providence and our own labor. Jesus didn't tell us to ask the Lord for our daily bread so that we can sleep in each morning and make no effort to bring forth the fruit of honest labor. On the contrary, God commands us to be productive in our labor and with respect to the provision of our daily needs. The apostle Paul tells us that "if anyone does not provide for his own, and especially for those of his household, he has denied the faith and is worse than an unbeliever" (1 Tim. 5:8). So on the one hand, we have to trust in the benevolent providence of God to give us our daily bread, and on the other hand, we are to be industrious, doing all that we can to provide for our families. God typically works through means, and He normally provides through the means of our labor.

Trusting God from Day to Day

Second, notice that when we ask God to give us our bread, we are not to request that He provide it weekly or monthly, but *daily*. We are to ask for a day's worth of bread at a time.

I moved my family to Holland for a time when I was working on my doctorate. We lived out in a village where hardly anyone spoke English, so we were forced to pick up some rudimentary Dutch as quickly as we could. Sherrie, our daughter, was about three years old at the time, and the first Dutch word she learned was *snoepja*, which means a little piece of candy. That's the word all Dutch children learn first, I suppose. But the first basic sentence she learned didn't have to do with candy. There would be a knock on the door every morning as the baker arrived, and it was Sherrie's job to answer the door. She would look at the baker and say, "Dag mijnheer bakker, een halfje gesneden brood alstublieft." That meant, "Good morning, Mr. Baker, a half a loaf of sliced bread, please." That's the first basic sentence she learned to speak, and she mastered it in no time because she said it *every day*. You see, in Holland at that time, you didn't go to the store and buy a loaf of bread, bring it home, and use it for the week. The bread that was available—which, by the way, was the most fabulous bread I've ever eaten—had to be delivered every day. There were no preservatives in it, so after a day, it was virtually inedible. So we had to have fresh bread each day.

Why does Jesus place such emphasis on *daily* bread? I doubt it had anything to do with the lack of preservatives in the bread at the time. Rather, I believe Jesus had a much more profound reason for instructing us to request daily bread. I think He did so primarily to teach us that we need to acknowledge our dependence on the providence of God to sustain us day to day. He was saying that we should live in a daily dependence on the provision that God gives.

This was a recurring theme in the teaching of Jesus. In the same Sermon on the Mount where Jesus taught the Lord's Prayer, He also said:

> "Do not worry about your life, what you will eat or what you will drink; nor about your body, what you will put on. . . . Look at the birds of the air, for they neither sow nor reap nor gather into barns; yet your heavenly Father feeds them. Are you not of more value than they? . . . Consider the lilies of the field, how they grow: they neither toil nor spin; and yet I say to you that even Solomon in all his glory was not arrayed like one of these. Now if God so clothes the grass of the field, which today is, and tomorrow is thrown into the oven, will He not much more clothe you, O you of little faith? . . . Therefore do not worry about tomorrow." (Matt. 6:25–34a)

In that same context, Jesus also said: "What man is there among you who, if his son asks for bread, will give him a stone? Or if he asks for a fish, will he give him a serpent? If you then, being evil, know how to give good gifts to your children, how much more will your Father who is in heaven give good things to those who ask Him!" (Matt. 7:9–11). God, Jesus taught, gives perfect gifts, and He is willing and able to meet our daily needs, which we are to bring before Him on a daily basis.

We have a tendency in this modern age *not* to live from day to day in terms of the things we need to eat. We stock up on food. We have refrigerators and freezers that extend the life of our food and keep it fresh. So it's not our custom to face each new day with the fresh need to find food for our sustenance. Given this custom, we have a powerful need to pray this petition of the Lord's Prayer and to grasp our constant dependence on the provision of God to sustain our very lives.

Bread from Heaven

Third, Jesus teaches us to pray that God would give us daily *bread*. Obviously Jesus was not telling His disciples to pray only for bread. But bread was a staple in the diet of the Jews, and had been so for many years. Furthermore, bread was a powerful symbol of God's provision for His people in the Old Testament. We remember how God cared for the Israelites when they were in the wilderness after their exodus from Egypt. Life in the wilderness was hard, and soon the people began to complain that it would be better to be back in Egypt, where they had wonderful food to eat. In response to these complaints, God promised to "rain bread from heaven" (Ex. 16:4). The next morning, when the dew lifted, there remained behind on the ground "a small round substance, as fine as frost. . . . It was like white coriander seed, and the taste of it was like wafers made with honey" (vv. 14, 31). When God miraculously fed His people from heaven, he did so by giving them bread.

It's interesting to me that in the language of Western culture, we sometimes speak of one partner in a marriage (it used to be almost exclusively the husband, but not so much these days) as the wage earner of the home. But more colloquially, we call that partner "the breadwinner." Even in our slang, we use the word *bread* as a synonym for "money." Bread remains, at least in our language, as a powerful symbol of the rudimentary basis of provision for our needs.

After the Korean War ended, South Korea was left with a large number of children who had been orphaned by the war. We've seen the same thing in the Vietnam conflict, in Bosnia, and in other places. In the case of Korea, relief agencies came in to deal with all the problems that arose in connection with having so many orphan children. One of the people involved in this relief effort told me about a problem they encountered with the children who were in the orphanages. Even though the children had three meals a day provided for them, they were restless and anxious at night and had difficulty sleeping. As they talked to the children, they soon discovered that the children had great anxiety about whether they would have food the next day. To help resolve this problem, the relief workers in one particular orphanage decided that each night when the children were put to bed, the nurses there would place a single piece of bread in each child's hand. The bread wasn't intended to be eaten; it was simply intended to be held by the children as they went to sleep. It was a "security blanket" for them, reminding them that there would be provision for their daily needs. Sure enough, the bread calmed the children's anxieties and helped them sleep. Likewise, we take comfort in knowing that our physical needs are met, that we have food, or "bread," for our needs.

This petition of the Lord's Prayer, then, teaches us to come to God in a spirit of humble dependence, asking Him to provide what we need and to sustain us from day to day. We are not given license to ask for great riches, but we are encouraged to make our needs known to Him, trusting that He will provide.

If we find that God's hand seems to be invisible to us and that we cannot discern His providential intrusion into our lives, that may be due partly to the way we pray. We have a tendency to pray in general. When we pray in general, the only way we will see the hand of God's providence is in general. As we enter into prayer, this conversation and communion with God, and put our petitions before Him, pouring out our souls and our needs specifically, we see specific answers to our prayers. Our Father has invited us to go to Him and ask Him for our daily bread. He will not fail to provide it.

SEVEN

Forgive Us Our Debts

I once saw a report about a study of guilt complexes among students at various universities and colleges. The study was designed to reveal the anxiety levels of people with respect to unresolved guilt problems. One of the schools in this study was a Christian college, and to my astonishment, the students at this college ranked in the ninety-ninth percentile of people who are walking around with unresolved guilt. I couldn't help wondering how it could be that students at a Christian college would have such a high degree of guilt. If any people should have freedom from guilt, it should be Christians, for Christians understand grace, the cross, and the Father's forgiveness of our sins.

I suppose part of the explanation for the results uncovered by this study is that in the secular colleges people have so repressed their guilt feelings that they don't feel all that bad about their behavior. When a person becomes a Christian, he or she becomes more sensitive to the obligation we have to obey God, and so his or her conscience can be more easily troubled. Still, something seems wrong here. If these students had been following Jesus' mandate in the Lord's Prayer, I don't believe they would have had so much guilt on their hearts.

I'm thinking, of course, of the fifth petition of the Lord's Prayer, where Jesus taught His disciples to say, "Forgive us our debts, as we forgive our debtors" (Matt. 6:12). As I mentioned in the previous chapter when I discussed the A-C-T-S acrostic, which serves to help us remember the elements of prayer and their proper priority, confession of sin is to be a regular part of our prayer lives, and so it is no surprise that we find Jesus teaching us to seek the Father's forgiveness.

The text of the fifth petition that I cited above is taken from the New King James Version. Like the NKJV, most English translations of the Scriptures use the word *debts* here in Matthew 6:12. However, in some churches, when the Lord's Prayer is recited, a slightly different wording is used: "Forgive us our trespasses, as we forgive those who trespass against us." Which of these options, *debts* or *trespasses*, is the correct one? The answer, of course, is either. Both *debts* and *trespasses* are accurate synonyms for the word *sins*, which is what Jesus is addressing here.

In Debt to God

Nevertheless, *debts* is a good word choice here, because when the New Testament addresses sin, one of the main ways in which sin is described is as a debt. When we sin, we put ourselves into debt to God; we incur an obligation; we come to owe Him something. Thus, when we ask for His forgiveness, we are asking that He forgive our debt.

We usually think of debt in monetary terms. However, there are also moral debts. Imagine a little boy who walks into an ice cream parlor and orders an ice cream cone with two scoops. The waitress dutifully prepares his ice cream cone, then says, "That will be two dollars." When he hears this, the little boy begins to cry. He looks helplessly to the waitress and says, "But my Mommy only gave me one dollar." What would you do if you saw this taking place? You would do what anyone would do—you would say, "Let me satisfy the young man's debt," then you would reach into your pocket, take out some money, and pay the waitress the extra dollar. Since the money you are offering is legal tender, the waitress would have to accept that in payment, and the little boy could then go home and enjoy his ice cream cone.

But suppose that when the little boy was told his ice cream cone would cost $2 he turned and ran from the store without paying—right into the arms of a police officer on his beat while the waitress is crying out, "Stop, thief." The officer would bring the boy back into the store and ask the waitress what had happened, and she would explain that the boy had just stolen the ice cream cone. Once again, you see all this happen, so you say, "Wait a minute, officer, please don't put this boy in jail, I'll pay for his cone." In this scenario, the waitress does not have to accept your money because now the boy has a moral debt, not just a monetary debt.

The distinction between a monetary debt and a moral debt is

important because it can give us a deeper understanding of what took place on the cross. When we sinned, we fell into a moral debt to God. Jesus paid our debt at the cross, but because it was a moral debt, the Father was not required to accept the Son's payment. However, in His mercy and His grace, He allowed Jesus to pay our moral debt.

An Impossible Debt

We need to be eternally thankful that the Son stepped in to pay our debt to the Father, for as the Bible also makes clear, our debt was so great we could not possibly pay it. If someone told me I owed him $10,000 and I would have to go to jail unless I came up with it within a week, I think I could find the money so I could keep myself out of jail. But if the person were to say that I owed him $10 billion, my situation would be hopeless. I don't think the combined assets of all the people I know would amount to $10 billion. But our moral obligation to God is far greater than a $10 billion monetary debt.

What is the nature of our debt to God? He has commanded us to be holy, even as He is holy; to be perfect, even as He is perfect. With one sin, one transgression, we fall hopelessly short of that standard, placing ourselves in a position of indebtedness we can never escape. You've heard the adage that everyone's entitled to one mistake. That's part of the entitlement mentality of the United States, where we think we have rights to all kinds of things. In truth, the only thing we're entitled to is everlasting punishment in hell. God never said we are entitled to one mistake, and if we were, how long ago did each of us use up our one mistake? We have sinned against God and His perfect holiness multiple times since we got out of our beds this morning. How great is our debt after a lifetime of sin?

The apostle Paul, speaking about unbelievers, said, "In accordance with your hardness and your impenitent heart, you are treasuring up for yourself wrath in the day of wrath and revelation of the righteous judgment of God" (Rom. 2:5). Paul was saying that every day a person lingers in this life without falling on his knees and asking God to forgive his debts, he is increasing that "treasury of wrath." The problem is that the mercy and patience of God convince impenitent people that since they have escaped the judgment of God so far, they will escape it forever. These are the kinds of people who say to me again and again, "It's nice that you're a Christian, but I don't feel the need for Jesus." When I hear that, I want to weep. I want to say: "Don't you understand that what you need more desperately than anything in the world is Jesus? Don't you feel the weight of that debt that you can't possibly pay?" I want to help them see that when that debt is called, it will be the most severe crisis they have ever faced, for they won't be able to pay.

Jesus loved people enough to warn them and to teach them to beg God for forgiveness. That's why Jesus said, "In this manner, therefore, pray: . . . Forgive us our debts."

Sin as Crime and Enmity

As I mentioned, one of the main ways in which the New Testament describes sin is as a debt. But it also speaks of sin as a crime and as a state of enmity. I believe it is worth considering these descriptions of sin briefly so that we understand what is at stake when we come to the Father to seek His forgiveness.

First, sin is described as a crime. Imagine a man who is brought to trial on charges of first-degree murder. When he was arrested, he was holding a smoking gun. A video camera recorded his bloody act. Witnesses are ready to testify that, before the crime, he boasted of his intent to murder. All the evidence indicates the guilt of the accused, but when he is asked for his plea, he says, "Not guilty." He then says to the judge, "I can't be guilty because I don't feel guilty." Is the judge likely to heed such a defense? No. The question of the accused man's guilt is not a question of feeling. It is something objective, not something subjective. It is a question of whether that person has, in fact, broken the law.

The Westminster Shorter Catechism asks, "What is sin?" It then answers, "Sin is any want of conformity to, or transgression of, the law of God" (Q/A 14). Sin, therefore, is a transgression or violation of the law. If a proven violation of man's law constitutes a crime, so does a proven violation of God's law.

Scripture often describes God as the Judge. He certainly will not judge us by our feelings. He will judge us by His law. His judgment will be perfect, absolutely just. He must punish violations of His law. Thus, we will certainly be found guilty of our crimes—unless someone else acts as a substitute for us, to take the penalty we deserve.

Second, sin is described as a state of enmity or estrangement. Human beings, by nature, are the enemies of God. In our natural state, Scripture tells us, we are estranged from our heavenly Father, the one who made us and sustains us. People may not think they bear any hostility toward Him, but the Bible makes it clear that in our hearts, prior to our regeneration, we hate Him. We need to be reconciled to Him. We need to be at peace with Him.

Why Do Men Hate God?

Many years ago, I read a sermon by Jonathan Edwards titled "Men Naturally Are God's Enemies." In that sermon, which was based on Romans 5:10, Edwards explored the reasons we are hostile toward God. He identified a few aspects of God's nature that provoke hostility within us.

First and foremost, God is holy and we are not. People who are not holy do not appreciate a standard that reveals their unrighteousness. If God were not so holy, and we were not so sinful, perhaps we could get along. But God's perfect holiness and our sinfulness combine to create a breach we cannot close. It can be closed only by the mediating work of the Savior, who offers forgiveness for our sin.

Second, God is omniscient. Because God sees and knows all, we cannot hide from Him. We can hide from the gaze of humans in our private sin, but there is no way to avoid the gaze of God. When I was a little boy, my mother worked at the office with my father, and I had a lot of free time without supervision. She would say to me, "I can't watch you today, but God's watching you." It was worse than Santa Claus making his list and checking it twice. Well, I grew up and went to college, went to seminary, and did doctoral studies, so I learned some theology. In time, I realized that the simple way in which my mother talked about God looking at me all the time was exactly right. Nothing escapes His notice. As David said, "Where can I go from Your Spirit? Or where can I flee from your presence? If I ascend into heaven, You are there; if I make my bed in hell, behold, You are there" (Ps. 139:7–8). Likewise, Jesus said we will have to give account for every "idle word" we speak (Matt. 12:36). God will be able to require this account because He knows every idle word that falls from our lips. I can imagine standing before the bar of God's justice and hearing a recording of every offensive thing I've ever said. I don't want that to happen. I want my sin to be covered long before I get to that point.

Third, God is omnipotent. If He were holy and knew everything about us but was impotent, we would have nothing to worry about. But He is all-powerful; there is no force in heaven or on earth that can subdue His strength. As the psalmist declares: "The kings of the world set themselves, and the rulers take counsel together, against the Lord and against His Anointed, saying, 'Let us break Their bonds in pieces and cast away Their cords from us.' He who sits in the heavens shall laugh; the Lord shall hold them in derision" (Ps. 2:2–4). The plots against the sovereignty of God were so useless as to be laughable. Jeremiah wrote, "O Lord, You induced me, and I was persuaded; You are stronger than I, and have prevailed" (20:7a). If God puts forth His strength, He will prevail. Nothing can defeat the power of God.

Fourth, God is immutable. He does not change. When I read this point in Edwards' sermon, I thought to myself, I can understand why we don't like God's holiness, omniscience, and power, but what would make me be hostile toward His immutability? Edwards anticipated my mystification. He noted that God's immutability means that not only has He been absolutely holy from everlasting to everlasting, there is no hope that He will ever stop being holy. Sometimes we root for righteous people to fail, so that we won't be embarrassed by their excellence. God's holiness, by contrast, is an immutable holiness. He will never cease to be anything other than perfectly holy.

Neither can we hope that God's omniscience will fail Him someday. God promised through Jeremiah that "I will forgive their iniquity, and their sin I will remember no more" (31:34b). We sometimes think this kind of statement means God "forgives and forgets," that once He's forgiven us, He never recalls that we once sinned. That's not what this passage means at all. God knows every sin I've ever committed and every sin of mine He's ever forgiven, and He will always have that knowledge, because His knowledge is immutable. When the Bible speaks of God forgetting our sins, it means that He remembers them *against us* no more. Though He's fully aware of our transgressions, He doesn't remind us, He doesn't call them to mind, He doesn't hold them against us. That's the essence of forgiveness, and we need to imitate that in this world. When I say to someone, "I forgive you," I am making a commitment to that person never to bring it up again.

Finally, there's no hope that God will ever lose any of His power. His right arm will not wither. He always will be omnipotent.

This all teaches us what a formidable opponent God is. When we are hostile toward Him, when we are estranged from Him, we've entered a battle we cannot possibly win. The only way the battle can end is by our unconditional surrender. That's what I do when I get on my knees and say, "Forgive me my debts." I'm giving up. I'm saying: "God, I can't fight You. I don't want to be estranged from You. I want to be restored to You. I want to be able to love You, not hate You. I want You to love me, in spite of my hostility toward You." Praying the fifth petition of the Lord's Prayer is to sue for peace.

A Frightening Condition

Notice, however, that Jesus attaches a condition to this petition. He doesn't simply tell us to pray, "Forgive us our debts." Rather, we are to ask God to forgive us "as we forgive our debtors." In my opinion, that's one of the most frightening lines in the Lord's Prayer. If this condition is to be taken literally, we are finished. Manifestly, if God forgave me in exact proportion to the manner in which I distribute forgiveness to other people, I would perish. I just cannot be as forgiving as God; none of us can. But thank God that this is an aspiration rather than a condition, that Jesus is teaching us to aspire to mirror and reflect the kindness of God, to stand ready to forgive anyone who has sinned against us or offended us when they repent.

Jesus makes this point in His parables, stressing that since we are forgiven much, we should have a deep spirit of charity toward other people. How can we refuse to forgive someone who has offended us when the whole reason we are able to live in the kingdom of God is that we have received forgiveness? Forgiveness is the only way we can stand in the presence of God. Since God is willing to forgive us when we have sinned so much more radically and egregiously against Him than anyone has ever sinned against us, how can we not be willing to forgive?

There is a warning I want to give. I think there's a serious misunderstanding in the Christian world about forgiveness. So often I hear people say that if anyone sins against you, you are required by God to forgive him or her unilaterally and immediately, whether the person repents or not. I don't find that in the Scriptures, though I do see Jesus doing that, when He prayed for the forgiveness of His executioners even though they had not repented. Of course, we may forgive those who have offended us without their repentance. We are not to be vindictive or vengeful in our attitudes, and if someone harms me, I should be ready and willing to absorb it in the name of love. However, there are injuries that are so serious that there are provisions both in the Old Testament and the New Testament to involve the church authorities. If someone sins against you, and you go to see that person to try to bring about reconciliation but he or she refuses to repent, there's a process that you are to follow. You are to take another person with you to see the offending person, then, if necessary, appeal to the church (Matt. 18:15–17).

It is at this point that church discipline occurs. Church courts exist to settle grievances and to bring justice to the relationships among Christians. If we are obligated in every situation to forgive immediately, directly, and unilaterally, there is no need for the whole process of discipline in the church. Since God gives these measures of discipline to the church, I think it follows that we are not absolutely obligated to forgive everyone who sins against us if they remain impenitent.

The point is that I should be as gracious toward others as God has been to me, so that if someone does sin against me and then he acknowledges his guilt, repents, and apologizes, I am duty bound to forgive. Jesus said we are to forgive our brothers "seventy times seven" (Matt. 18:22) if they sin against us that many times. If they keep repenting over and over again, we have to keep forgiving over and over again, because that's the basic relationship that we have with God.

Still, as I said, it is terrifying to pray, "O God, please forgive me proportionately to the way in which I forgive people who have offended me." That scares me, because I know I have not been anywhere near as gracious in dealing with people who have offended me as God has been in dealing with me, nor am I capable of being so gracious. I will be in deep trouble if God provides forgiveness for me only to the degree that I am willing to provide it to others.

This petition, then, reminds us of the depth of our sinfulness, our need for daily confession, and our need for forgiveness, but also of our Christian duty in our interpersonal relationships on the human level. We are to keep short accounts not just in our vertical relationship with God, but in our horizontal relationships with others.

Yes, my sins have all been paid for, once and for all, on the cross. But Jesus taught us to pray for forgiveness as part of our ongoing communion with God. We need a fresh understanding, a fresh experience, of His grace and of His forgiveness every day. There is no greater state than to get up from your knees knowing that in God's sight you are clean, that He has forgiven every sin you've ever committed. Without that grace, without that forgiveness, I don't think I could live in this world for another sixty seconds. This is something we all desperately need, and we have but to ask for it.

EIGHT

Do Not Lead Us into Temptation

Having taught His disciples how to deal with their past sins in the fifth petition of the Lord's Prayer—"Forgive us our debts, as we forgive our debtors"—Jesus turned His attention from the past to the future and addressed their vulnerability to sins beyond today and into tomorrow. By teaching His followers to ask, "Do not lead us into temptation, but deliver us from the evil one" (Matt. 6:13a), Jesus showed that we are to ask the Father to spare us from the temptations and the spiritual attacks that can lead us into new sin.

A superficial reading of this petition of the Lord's Prayer should jar our sensibilities to some degree, because nothing could be farther from the realm of possibility than that God would entice anyone to sin. James teaches in his epistle, "Let no one say when he is tempted, 'I am tempted by God'; for God cannot be tempted by evil, nor does He Himself tempt anyone" (1:13). James goes on to explain that enticement and temptation to sin arise from within, from our own evil inclinations and desires. External temptations can come to us from fellow sinners who want misery in company or from Satan himself, who is known in the Bible as the tempter. But God Himself does not engage in temptation to sin. How, then, are we to understand this petition?

The force of the language does not have to do with God's enticing us to sin. A better wording might be, "Do not lead us into the place of testing." Jesus is saying that we should pray that the Father will never cause us to undergo a severe test of our faith or of our obedience.

God, however, sometimes deems it best for His children to go through testing. For this reason, we see examples in Scripture of God delivering someone to be tested, to go through trials in order to purify that person's faith and to refine his or her righteousness. Consider Abraham, who was put to that abysmal test that is recorded in Genesis 22. For many years, hoping against hope, believing against all things that were seen, Abraham hung tenaciously to God's promise that he would have a son from his own body and that he eventually would be the father of a great nation. Finally, in his old age, God fulfilled His promise, and the child of promise, Isaac, was born. But one dreadful day, God put Abraham to the test. God came to him and said, "Take now your son, your only son Isaac, whom you love, and go to the land of Moriah, and offer him there as a burnt offering on one of the mountains of which I shall tell you" (Gen. 22:2). Abraham obeyed all that God told him to do, to the point of raising his knife to slay Isaac on the altar. But at the last possible second, God sent an angel crying out, "Abraham, Abraham! . . . Do not lay your hand on the lad, or do anything to him; for now I know that you fear God, since you have not withheld your son, your only son, from me" (22:11b–12). Abraham had passed his test. He then turned and saw a ram caught in the thicket by its horns. God was *Jehovah Jireh*, the God who provides. He had provided a substitute to be slain in the place of Abraham's son.

A Specific Evil

Jesus does not simply teach us to pray that God would deliver us from testing. He gets very specific in the second part of the sixth petition. This part of the petition both reinforces and expands what Jesus is teaching us in this petition, for we find here a Hebrew literary strategy called parallelism, a technique that links two statements so that the second illumines the significance of the first.

This petition is frequently translated and recited with these words: "Lead us not into temptation, but deliver us from evil." The use of the word *evil* in this translation is not accurate, and it often causes a lot of misunderstanding. People come to all sorts of incorrect ideas about what "evil" means, but the original Greek makes the meaning perfectly clear.

In the Scriptures, in the New Testament Greek, the word for evil is *poneron*. The last two letters, *-on*, indicate something particular. In the Greek language, as in many languages, nouns can be masculine, feminine, or neuter. We sometimes do this even in English when we talk about ships or even cars and call them by feminine pronouns. Well, the *-on* ending puts this Greek word in the neuter form. In this form, it refers to evil in the abstract. But this is not the form in which the word appears in the Lord's Prayer. Here, the Greek word is not *poneron*, it's *poneros*—and the *-os* ending in the Greek indicates a masculine noun. Therefore, what Jesus is saying here is best translated not as "deliver us from evil" but as "deliver us from the evil one." The New King James Version has it exactly right, for when the term *poneros* is used in the New Testament, it is a title specifically for Satan.

Now we can see how the second half of this petition amplifies the first. As Scripture reveals, God often uses Satan to bring testing on His children. Thus, when Jesus teaches us to pray, "Do not lead us into temptation, but deliver us from the evil one," He not only is teaching us to pray for deliverance from testing, but teaching us to seek divine protection from the wiles of Satan. He is calling us to pray that we would not be exposed to the Devil's onslaughts, to his attempts to entice us to sin or to destroy our confidence in our Savior by accusing us of our failures and of our imperfections.

Biblical Tests of Faith

Let's look at some of the biblical narratives in which we find Satan being used in the testing of individuals. First, let's go back to the creation story, to the pristine purity our primordial parents enjoyed in the Garden of Eden. Adam and Eve were created and lived initially without sin, in a state of innocence, but the opening words of Genesis 3 are ominous. They are filled with a sense of foreboding, as something dark and sinister is introduced to redemptive history with the seemingly innocuous words, "Now the serpent was more cunning than any beasts of the field which the Lord God had made" (v. 1a). What follows in this narrative is the attempt by the serpent, who is Satan, to persuade Adam and Eve to follow him rather than their Creator. He comes to them with a simple question about God's authority: "Has God indeed said, 'You shall not eat of every tree of the garden?'" (v. 1b). When Eve answers the serpent and mentions that death is the penalty God has assigned for eating from the tree of the knowledge of good and evil, Satan then launches a frontal assault: "You will not surely die. For God knows that in the day you eat of it your eyes will be opened, and you will be like God, knowing good and evil" (v. 4a). In other words, Satan says: "God didn't tell you the truth. Don't believe Him. Believe *me*."

The backdrop to this encounter is the probationary status of Adam and Eve. God had given them a promise of life contingent on their obedience to His one command. They were not to eat the fruit of the tree of the knowledge of good and evil. When God allowed them to be tested, they failed. They succumbed to the subtle wiles of the evil one and plunged the entire human race into ruin and death. This was a monumental test, a supremely important trial, but Adam and Eve failed it miserably.

Fast forward to the patriarch Job, who though he was a member of the fallen race of Adam, nevertheless distinguished himself by his extraordinary righteousness and obedience. Satan, we are told, comes to heaven after walking to and fro across the earth.

In that encounter, God asks whether Satan, in his wanderings, had taken notice of Job. God adds, "There is none like him on the earth, a blameless and upright man, one who fears God and shuns evil" (Job 1:8b). Satan responds with sneering contempt: "Does Job fear God for nothing? Have You not made a hedge around him? . . . You have blessed the work of his hands, and his possessions have increased in the land. But now, stretch out Your hand and touch all that he has, and he will surely curse You to Your face!" (vv. 9b–11). God says, "Behold, all that he has is in your power; only do not lay a hand on his person" (v. 12). God tells Satan, "You can take his wealth, you can take his property, you can take his good name, his reputation, his family, you can afflict him any way you want, but you can't make him suffer physically." Satan doesn't hold back. If any man in the history of the world is subjected to every dreadful attack that Satan could make, it is Job. His livestock, his servants, and his children all are taken away, but Job refuses to find fault with God's providence.

That leads to Satan's second visit to heaven, where he once again discusses Job with God. God mentions that Job "holds fast to his integrity, although you incited Me against him, to destroy him without cause" (2:3b). To that, Satan replies that Job would curse God if he were to suffer in his body. Once again God acquiesces and once again Satan goes after Job with all his fury, so that Job is afflicted with boils all over his body. In the midst of his hellish suffering, Job's wife, who no doubt loves and cares for him, and who wants to comfort him and release him from his pain, becomes an instrument of the serpent. She says, "Do you still hold fast to your integrity? Curse God and die!"

(2:9). Job can hardly speak, but he says, "Shall we indeed accept good from God, and shall we not accept adversity?" (2:10b). Later, as Job endures the "comforts" of his friends, he makes an even more powerful statement of his trust in God: "Though He slay me, yet will I trust Him" (13:15a). That's what it means to be a servant of God. Job aced the test, and God blessed him and restored the things he had lost.

The worst test ever endured by a human being was the one given to the God-man, the Lord Jesus Christ. Immediately after His baptism, the Spirit of God drove Him into the Judean wilderness, to be tempted by the Devil for forty days. We have no idea of what our Lord endured in that time alone in the wilderness. Whereas the first Adam fell to a simple seductive suggestion, the new Adam endured everything that hell could throw at Him. Satan tempted Jesus in manifold ways, but Jesus answered each temptation with Scripture and so turned back all the assaults. But the test didn't end when the forty days were finished. The Devil finally left Jesus, but Luke adds, he left only "until an opportune time" (4:13b). Satan kept coming back to try to cause Jesus to stumble, to try to make Him fall.

When Jesus instructed His disciples to pray, "Do not lead us into temptation, but deliver us from the evil one," He was speaking from experience. He had passed through a time of testing at the hands of Satan, so He instructed His disciples to ask the Father to spare them from the Devil's attacks. He was teaching His followers to pray, "O Lord, don't expose us to the place of temptation where we are going to be assaulted by the power of Satan, but protect us from his fiery darts. Place a hedge around us. Be our shields." We should pray every day for deliverance, not in the sense of demon exorcism, but in the sense of protection from the assaults of Satan.

None of us has ever been tested like Abraham, like Adam and Eve, like Job, or like our Lord. Yet, church history is replete with examples of Christians being put to the test, even to the point of martyrdom. We can find many examples of God calling believers to endure the worst, then giving them the grace to endure it. For instance, in the second century, Polycarp, the aged bishop of Smyrna, was taken into Roman custody and told he must renounce Christ or be killed. Polycarp replied, "Eighty-six years I have served Him, and He never once wronged me. How can I blaspheme my King, who saved me?" He was martyred a few moments later. Likewise, Bishops Hugh Latimer and Nicholas Ridley were burned at the stake during the persecutions of "Bloody" Queen Mary for teaching justification by faith alone. As the fire was being lit, Latimer called: "Be of good cheer, Master Ridley, and play the man. We shall this day light such a candle in England by God's grace as, I trust, shall never be put out." So it has been through the centuries, as Christians have gone through deep testing.

The Devil's Accusations

We're familiar with the role of Satan as the tempter, and that's certainly his stock-in-trade. But if anything is his trademark in terms of the work he does in the life of the Christian, it's not so much the work of temptation as the work of accusation. Satan seeks to do everything he can to paralyze believers with unresolved guilt. In that sense, he's standing in direct opposition to the truth of God, which, of course, has been his role from the beginning. Ever since Eden, Satan has been about contradicting what God says.

God makes a simple but profound promise to Christians: "If we confess our sins, He is faithful and just to forgive us our sins and to cleanse us from all unrighteousness" (1 John 1:9). When a child of God confesses his sin, God forgives it—it's as simple as that. But as soon as God says that believer is forgiven, Satan shows up and says: "Oh, no, you're not. You are still guilty." When a Christian listens to him, he become burdened and weighed down with a paralyzing load of guilt. That guilt, in turn, robs the believer of his assurance of salvation.

Paul addresses this problem when he writes, almost triumphantly: "Who shall bring a charge against God's elect? It is God who justifies. Who is he who condemns?" (Rom. 8:33–34a). God has justified us on the basis of the righteousness of Christ. Thus, when Satan brings his accusations against us, we should respond: "Yes, Satan, I sinned, but now my guilt is covered and my sin is washed away. Be gone!"

Peter referred to Satan as the believer's "adversary" (1 Peter 5:8). But we are assured that if we "resist the devil . . . he will flee" (James 4:7), and prayer is a key weapon in our resistance. Martin Luther is a powerful example to us in this. Luther had an acute awareness of the presence of Satan. On one occasion, he threw his inkwell across the room, saying he had seen Satan there. He spoke of the *anfectung*, Satan's unbridled assault against him to try to make him compromise, fall into despair, or deny the faith. In this struggle, Luther resorted to prayer, and he went to his knees every day to pray the Lord's Prayer, specifically the sixth petition: "Do not lead us into temptation, but deliver us from the evil one."

I often ask myself how I would measure up if God allowed me to be severely tested. I honestly don't know, and I don't want to have to find out. So I often pray this petition of the Lord's Prayer, asking: "O Lord, please, please, keep that hedge around me. Don't put me in that place of testing. Deliver me from the evil one, who goes about like a roaring lion, ready to devour whomever he will." I pray for divine protection from all the forces of evil that surround us, and I believe this petition should be on every believer's lips each day.

NINE

Yours Is the Kingdom

Recently, as I was preparing to preach a sermon on the concluding line of the Lord's Prayer, I experienced no small amount of consternation. My normal procedure in sermon preparation is to look at the text carefully, look at it in the Greek, look at it in the Latin, and then consult four or five commentaries to see what insights I might gain from others who have studied the text. But as I studied for this particular sermon, I examined no fewer than ten commentaries and was astonished to discover that not a single one of them included more than two sentences about the conclusion to the Lord's Prayer. I was stunned by this lack of attention, because I think this is one of the most important portions of the Lord's Prayer, if not the most important.

I can point to at least one reason for this lack of scholarly attention—there's a textual problem involved. Many of the ancient manuscripts include this doxological ending to the prayer, but some do not, among them the *Codex Vaticanus*, which is one of the most important of the ancient texts. As a result, there is a widespread belief among scholars that this ending was not in the original prayer but was added very soon afterward because it was customary among the Jews to conclude their prayers with a doxology. But even the scholars who are convinced that this line was in the original prayer give little or no attention to it. Instead, they treat it as something of a postscript, sort of a throwaway line that isn't all that important, particularly in light of the significant petitions that precede it.

One of the most beautiful aspects of this concluding line of the Lord's Prayer, in my opinion, is that it returns the focus to God. As we saw in earlier chapters, the prayer opens with a strong Godward slant, as seen in the initial petitions: "Hallowed be Your name," "Your kingdom come," and "Your will be done." Jesus taught His disciples that their prayers should be centered on the glory of God, and it is only after we spend time praising and adoring Him that we should shift to focusing on our needs, through petitions such as "Give us this day our daily bread," "Forgive us our debts as we forgive our debtors," and "Do not lead us into temptation, but deliver us from the evil one." But at the end of the prayer, Jesus brings it full circle, and the focal point shifts from us back to God once again. The prayer ends with these words: "For Yours is the kingdom and the power and the glory forever. Amen" (Matt. 6:13b).

Things That Are God's

It is important to see that the pronoun that is used to identify God here, "Yours," is in the possessive form. With these words, believers affirm that the kingdom of heaven, supreme power, and ultimate glory all belong properly to God alone. So it has always been, so it is, and so it will be "forever."

Let us look more closely at these three things that Jesus says belong to God. First, we are to acknowledge that "the kingdom" is His. Manifestly, the kingdom of God is not my kingdom or your kingdom. It's His kingdom, His sovereign rule. He reigns supreme over all things and His kingdom shall have no end.

My local newspaper recently printed a quiz about the American Revolution and the founding of the United States. There were only ten questions in the quiz, but one of those questions really bugged me. It asked what kind of government the Founding Fathers established—an oligarchy, an aristocracy, an indirect democracy, or a direct democracy? I looked at that question and I asked myself, "Why didn't they give 'none of the above' as an option?" The United States of America was not founded as a democracy, either direct or indirect. It was founded as a republic, and there's a huge difference between the two. But the quiz also included a question about the thinkers who influenced the framers of the Declaration of Independence and the U.S. Constitution. The answer specifically mentioned the British empiricist John Locke, whose ideas, along with those of Thomas Hobbes and Edmund Burke, had a great influence. Locke's major contribution was in the area of the social contract of government, which states that people must agree to surrender some rights to government for the benefit of social order. This theory undergirds the idea that legitimate governmental authority stems from the consent of the governed. For this reason, the United States is said to have a government of the people, by the people, and for the people.

But not so the kingdom of God. The kingdom of God is not of the people, by the people, or for the people. It is a kingdom ruled by a King, and God does not rule by the consent of His subjects but by His sovereign authority. His reign extends over me whether I vote for Him or not.

The God of All Power

Second, Jesus teaches us that we should acknowledge in prayer that "the power" is God's. The Greek word that is translated as "power" here is *dunamis*. It's the same word from which we get the English word *dynamite*. This line of the Lord's Prayer reminds us that God possesses all power in heaven and on earth—power to create, power to save, and power to enable believers to live the Christian life.

I recently received a copy of Iain Murray's latest biography, an account of the life of D. Martyn Lloyd-Jones, one of the greatest preachers of the twentieth century. In this biography, Murray tells a story from the heyday of Lloyd-Jones' preaching career in London. There were three world-famous preachers in that city at that time, including Lloyd-Jones, and a visitor to London took the time to visit all three churches to personally hear each man preach. When he was finished with his survey, he said the first man preached the love of God, the second one preached Jesus, and the third, Lloyd-Jones, preached God. When I read that, I thought, "That's what preaching ought to be."

Murray notes that Lloyd-Jones said that no matter how disciplined a minister is in the preparation of his sermon, no matter how learned he may be, no matter how much knowledge he brings to the pulpit, no matter how eloquent and persuasive he is, without the accompanying power of God the Holy Spirit, his sermons are impotent. Lloyd-Jones was absolutely right, and I am acutely conscious of that. When I preach, if the Holy Spirit does not take the Word of God to my hearers' hearts, I am completely helpless, and I know it. That's why, at the beginning of each sermon, I ask God the Holy Spirit to descend and to help those in the congregation. That's not just a mere formal statement, it's a plea for my hearers. We all need the power of the Holy Spirit to bring the truth of the Word of God home to us. The Holy Spirit is sometimes called "the power of God," and that's the same word Jesus used in the Lord's Prayer, *dunamis.* He can take the Word of God and make it explode in a person's soul.

I think the greatest weakness in the church today is that almost no one believes that God invests His power in the Bible. Everyone is looking for power in a program, in a methodology, in a technique, in anything and everything but that in which God has placed it—His Word. He alone has the power to change lives for eternity, and that power is focused on the Scriptures.

Glory to God Alone

Third, Jesus instructs us to affirm in prayer that the glory is rightfully God's. In his great doxology in Romans 11, Paul does just that, declaring, "For of Him and through Him and to Him are all things, to whom be glory forever" (v. 36). Paul writes that all things are "of" God, "through" God, and "to" God, magnifying His glory forever. As servants of God, we should desire that He be magnified over all things, including ourselves. Our prayer should be that of John the Baptist: "He must increase, but I must decrease" (John 3:30).

It was the habit of Johann Sebastian Bach to write, at the bottom of each of his musical compositions, the initials "S.D.G." to remind himself and everyone who played his compositions that the glory was God's alone. "S.D.G.," of course, stands for the Latin phrase *Soli Deo gloria*, which means "Glory to God alone." Bach didn't write simply "D.G."—"Glory to God." It always had to be "S.D.G."—"Glory to God *alone*." That's what we affirm at the end of the Lord's Prayer. We acknowledge that we have no glory in us, that God is glorious beyond our ability to express, and that He is never required to share His glory with men.

The original temptation in Eden was to usurp the glory of God. The serpent said to Eve: "You will not surely die. For God knows that in the day you eat of it your eyes will be opened, and you will be like God, knowing good and evil" (Gen. 3:4). Satan's lie was that man would participate in deity. That lie is still being circulated today, tempting individuals to pursue ultimate glory. Yes, we should strive for significance. Yes, we should strive to make our lives count, but the glory belongs to God alone.

Finally, how long does God rule His kingdom? What is the duration of His possession of almighty power? At what point in the future does He share His glory? Jesus answers all these questions in this final line of the Lord's Prayer: "Yours is the kingdom and the power and the glory *forever.*" God's sovereignty, omnipotence, and glory are not temporary things. They will last into eternity. From everlasting to everlasting, He is God. From everlasting to everlasting, it is His kingdom, His power, His glory.

The Lord's Prayer concludes with that simple word that is so familiar to us, the word we use to close all our prayers but hardly ever consider: *Amen.* This is an Old Testament word, derived from the Aramaic, that means "truly" or "so be it." Having prayed according to Jesus' instructions, we declare "so be it."

In 1 Chronicles 29, following David's instructions, the people of Israel brought offerings for the construction of the temple. When that great offering was gathered in, David stood before the people, but he did not praise them. Instead, he lifted his eyes to heaven and said, "Yours, O LORD, is the greatness, the power and the glory, the victory and the majesty; for all that is in heaven and in earth is Yours; Yours is the kingdom, O LORD, and You are exalted as head over all" (v. 11). David ascribed the kingdom, the power, and the glory to God. So we must do, every day of our lives.

TEN

Questions and Answers

In this final chapter, I would like to touch briefly on various other issues surrounding the practice of prayer and the Lord's Prayer specifically.

In Isaiah 38, we are told that God warned King Hezekiah that he was about to die. But when Hezekiah prayed, God gave him another fifteen years of life. What is this passage teaching us about how prayer affects God's providence?

When we talk about God's sovereign government over the affairs of men, we say that God has had a plan from eternity and has ordained all that comes to pass. We know this to be true because Scripture says that God has declared the end from the beginning (Isa. 46:10). But we also have to remember that God not only ordains the ends, He also ordains the means to those ends. He determines the way in which His purposes are worked out. From our perspective, it sometimes may seem as if God changes His mind, and this story about Hezekiah is one of those instances. But when we analyze this story in light of the full teaching of Scripture, not drawing doctrinal conclusions only from narratives but also using the didactic portions of Scripture, we must conclude that God doesn't repent as humans do and doesn't change His mind. We know that it was God's plan from the beginning that Hezekiah would live that additional fifteen years, but that he would gain that fifteen years through the means of prayer.

Does this mean that when God sent Isaiah to tell King Hezekiah that he was going to die that God was requiring Isaiah to prophesy something that wasn't really going to happen? Was Isaiah a false prophet because he predicted something that didn't come to pass? Isaiah brought a word of impending doom and judgment, which was the very kind of message the prophets often brought. Countless times in the Old Testament God announces that He is going to bring judgment on the people, but then the people repent and God does not visit His judgment. Again, it seems that God changes His mind in these instances or that the original announcement of judgment was false.

Through the centuries, orthodox Christianity has taught that such warnings from God contain an implicit conditional clause. Sometimes God will say, "Unless you repent, you will undergo judgment." Other times, He simply says, "You will undergo judgment." Though God may not choose to explicitly say "Unless you repent," it is understood that God always has the right of tempering His judgment with grace. God has said, "I will have mercy on whomever I will have mercy" (Rom. 9:15), and the "unless you repent" is implied whenever He threatens judgment. So I believe Hezekiah heard the unspoken condition, "*Unless you repent*, you will die."

Some of the people in the biblical narratives seem to bargain with God. For instance, Hezekiah reminds God of what a good king he has been. Is it proper to pray in this fashion?

Scripture is brutally honest with us, revealing the faults and vices of the saints, as well as their virtues. We see inappropriate conduct even from great men such as Abraham, Moses, and David. Thus, the fact that the Bible tells us that various men tried to bargain or negotiate with God should not communicate to us that this is the appropriate way to deal with Him. Scripture is simply revealing this common human tendency, not sanctioning it. The fact is, people do this all the time. I've found myself trying to make deals with God, saying, "God, if you'll just give me one more chance, I'll do this, this, this, and this." God doesn't listen to that kind of prayer, for we are in no position to bargain with Him. To attempt to do so is to insult His character.

Scripture also contains examples of people almost lashing out at God in prayer. Is it ever legitimate to complain to God or to express anger to God?

We have manifold references in Scripture to believers bitterly complaining and almost accusing God of unfairness or harshness. We sometimes look at these instances and think, "Well, if

Moses can do it, if Job can do it, then it must be my prerogative as a Christian to voice my bitterness and complaints."

But we need to notice not just the complaints the biblical saints sometimes make, but the responses God gives. Let's take Job's complaint as an example. As Job struggled with his afflictions, he found it impossible not to grumble that God would let one as righteous as he was suffer so greatly. Eventually, however, God answered Job's complaints with stern words: "Who is this who darkens counsel by words without knowledge? Now prepare yourself like a man; I will question you, and you shall answer Me" (Job 38:2–3). What did Job say? Did he continue to complain? No. Instead, he declared: "I have uttered what I did not understand, things too wonderful for me, which I did not know. . . . Therefore I abhor myself, and repent in dust and ashes" (42:3b, 6). He was severely rebuked for the attitude that he expressed to God. Likewise, Habakkuk the prophet complained bitterly that God was not being just by allowing wickedness to go unchecked. He demanded an answer from God, and when God gave it, Habakkuk said, "My body trembled; my lips quivered at the voice; rottenness entered my bones; and I trembled in myself" (Hab. 3:16a).

It's vital that we understand prayer in terms of the qualifications that are found throughout the Bible. By considering the scope of the Bible's teaching on this subject, we may conclude that it is acceptable to bring all our cares to God, including matters that may move us to frustration or anger. However, we must not come to God in a spirit of complaint or anger *against Him*, for it is never proper to accuse God of wrongdoing.

In this book, you make the point repeatedly that when we pray we must be mindful of who God is and who we are, that He is the Creator and we are the creatures. Today, however, there seems to be a significant movement in the evangelical church toward familiarity with God. How do we balance reverence for God with the biblical permission to address Him as "Abba, Father"?

There is a simple answer to this question, but implementing the answer is not simple at all. God is revealed to us in Scripture as our heavenly Father, and we have been granted the privilege to address Him as such. We may come to God and speak to Him in these terms of personal intimacy, in a familial way, for we are part of His family. However, we must keep the rest of the character of God in mind. We must always remember that this One whom we address as Father is holy. Unfortunately, we are living in one of the most narcissistic ages in the history of the church, so that we focus far too much attention on ourselves and not nearly enough on the majesty of God. I think the eclipsing and obscuring of the character of God produces the excessive familiarity with God that we see in the church, a familiarity that is not at all appropriate when we are dealing with the King of kings. So the key, I believe, is to remember that we may speak to God in familial terms but we must guard against overly familiar terms.

The Lord's Prayer is widely recited, but it is rarely treated as a model for prayer. In other words, evangelicals rarely seek to draw principles for prayer from the Lord's Prayer. Why is this?

The principles for prayer that we find in the Lord's Prayer are not obscure principles—they're found throughout the book of Psalms and indeed throughout the Scriptures. So I think the biggest problem we have in our time is a severe ignorance of the content of Scripture. Sadly, this is true even among evangelicals, who claim to revere the Word of God and elevate the authority of Scripture. We simply don't know what's in the Bible, so it's not surprising that we don't know what the Bible teaches about prayer.

Some years ago, I was involved in the revision of a seminary curriculum. As we went through that process, I kept asking what it was that our students, who would be ministers someday, needed most. I had read that a survey had found that 30 percent of the average minister's time is spent in administration. That's a disaster. That's not what the minister is called to do. The minister is called to preach, teach, and to equip the saints for ministry. He is to be the pastor, the spiritual leader of the people. If he is to do that well, he has to know the Bible. We need pastors who are equipped to teach the Bible and who have time to teach the Bible. That's the only way to overcome this prevailing ignorance of Scripture. Only when that happens will people begin to grasp the principles for prayer.

What is the ministry of the Holy Spirit in regard to our prayers?

When we pray, we speak with a lisp, as it were, because our prayers are so inadequate and incomprehensible. The Holy Spirit helps us to pray according to the Word of God. We greatly need His assistance and we should be very grateful for it.

If God Is Sovereign, Why Pray?

How does the sovereignty of God relate to our daily lives? We understand from Scripture that God is sovereign, that He rules and reigns over all things for His glory and the good of His people. We also understand, having studied the Lord's Prayer throughout this book, that God invites us to come to Him in prayer, bringing our petitions before Him.

As soon as we set these two ideas—the sovereignty of God and the prayers of His people—side by side, we run into a very sticky theological question. Objections are raised from every quarter. People say: "Wait a minute. If God is sovereign, that is, if He has ordained every detail of what is taking place in our lives, not only in the present but in the future, why should we bother with prayer? Furthermore, since the Bible tells us that 'all things work together for good to those who love God' (Rom. 8:28), shouldn't we content ourselves that what God has ordained is best? Isn't it really just an exercise in futility, and even arrogance, for us to presume to tell God what we need or what we would like to happen? If He ordains all things, and what He ordains is best, what purpose is served by praying to Him?"

John Calvin briefly discusses this question of the usefulness of prayer in light of God's sovereignty in his *Institutes of the Christian Religion*:

> But some will say, "Does He not know without a monitor, both what our difficulties are and what is meet for our interest, so that it seems in some measure superfluous to solicit Him by our prayers, as if He were winking or even sleeping until aroused by the sound of our voice." Those who argue in this way attend not to the end or the purpose for which the Lord taught us to pray. It was not so much for God's good, as it was for our good. (Book III, Chap. 20)

Calvin argues that prayer benefits us more than it benefits God. We can see this readily enough, at least for some of the elements of prayer. Consider, for instance, the elements of adoration and confession. God's existence is not dependent on our praises. He can get along without them. But we can't. Adoration is necessary for our spiritual growth. If we are to develop an intimate relationship with our heavenly Father, it is essential that we come to Him with words expressing reverence, adoration, and love. At the same time, it is necessary for us that we mention our sins before His throne. He knows what they are. In fact, He knows them more clearly and more comprehensively than we do. He gains nothing by our giving Him a recitation of our sins, but we need that act of contrition for the good of our souls.

The intricate problem of the relationship between the sovereignty of God and human prayers comes not at the point of adoration and confession, but at the point of intercession and supplication. When I see someone in need and begin to pray for that person, I am interceding for him. I offer my requests to God on that person's behalf, pleading for God to act in His mercy, to do something to change that person's situation. Furthermore, I do the same for my own needs, as I perceive them. However, the omniscient God already knows everyone's situation, having ordained it. Therefore, are these prayers of any value? More fundamentally, do these prayers work? Do they ultimately have any impact on my life and on the lives of others?

The Efficacy of Prayer

We have to guard against taking a fatalistic view of this matter of prayer. We cannot allow ourselves to dismiss prayer from our lives simply because it might not seem to have pragmatic value. Whether or not prayer works, we must engage in it, simply because God Himself commands us to do it. Even a cursory reading of the Bible, particularly the New Testament, reveals a deep emphasis on prayer, supplication, and intercession. It is inescapable that prayer is an expected activity for the people of God. Furthermore, our Lord Himself is the supreme model for us in all things, and He clearly made prayer a huge priority in His life. We can do no less.

But it is also true that Scripture teaches us that prayer does "work" in some sense. Let me cite three examples.

We all know that the apostle Peter boldly declared that he would never betray Jesus, that he was ready to go to prison and even to death for his Lord. But rather than praising Peter for his determination, Jesus rebuked him and said, "Assuredly, I say to you that this night, before the rooster crows, you will deny Me three times" (Matt. 26:34). Luke's account adds an interesting detail to this exchange. Jesus said: "Simon, Simon! Indeed, Satan has asked for you, that he may sift you as wheat. But I have prayed for you, that your faith should not fail; and when you have returned to Me, strengthen your brethren" (Luke 22:31–32). Jesus warned Peter that a time of "sifting" was coming in his life, that Satan was going to attack him. But Jesus was sure that Peter would turn from his sin and turn back to Jesus. How could Jesus be sure of that? Well, He had prayed for Peter, that Peter's faith would not be shaken. Jesus was right—Peter did indeed turn back to Jesus and he did much to strengthen the brethren. Jesus' prayer for Peter was effective.

Not only do we see the prayers of Jesus effecting change in this world, we also see the prayers of the saints working. In the early days of the church, Peter was thrown into prison, but the believers gathered for a season of intense prayer on his behalf. They poured out their hearts before God, begging God to somehow overcome the adversity of the situation and secure the release of Peter. You know what happened: While they were involved in this intense prayer, there was a knock at the door. They didn't want to be disturbed from their prayer time, so they sent the servant to the door. When she went to the door and asked who was knocking, Peter answered and the servant recognized his voice. Overjoyed, she left the door closed and ran to tell the others that Peter was outside. The disciples refused to believe it until they opened the door and saw Peter himself standing there. God answered the prayers of His people, delivering Peter from prison by the help of an angel, but when he appeared at the house where the believers were gathered, these people who had prayed so earnestly for his release were frightened and shocked that God had actually answered their prayer. That's the way we are so often; when God answers our prayers, we can hardly believe it.

Moving to a didactic passage, James strongly encourages the people of God to pray:

> Is anyone among you suffering? Let him pray. Is anyone cheerful? Let him sing psalms. Is anyone among you sick? Let him call for the elders of the church, and let them pray over him, anointing him with oil in the name of the Lord. And the prayer of faith will save the sick, and the Lord will raise him up. . . . Pray for one another, that you may be healed. The effective, fervent prayer of a righteous man avails much. (James 5:13–18)

After these stirring words, which strongly emphasize the effectiveness of prayer, James goes on to speak of the prophet

Elijah. He stresses that Elijah was a man just like we are—he wasn't a super-saint or a magician. However, his prayers were extremely powerful. He prayed that God would stop the rain, and no rain at all fell for three and a half years. Then he prayed that God would send rain, and torrents fell.

Given these scriptural passages, and the many, many more that clearly show that prayer does achieve things, we are not free to say: "Well, God is in control. He's sovereign, immutable, and omniscient, so whatever will be will be. There's no point in praying." Scripture universally and absolutely denies that conclusion. Instead, it affirms that prayer does effect change. God, in His sovereignty, responds to our prayers.

God's "Natural" Laws

Others have questioned the efficacy of prayer from a more naturalistic consideration. They put forward the idea that we live in a world that operates according to fixed natural laws. It has been fashionable, in the past century or two, to think of God as merely the Architect and Creator of the universe, who set the universe in motion and decreed how it should operate, then stepped back and let it run without His direct involvement. This idea is almost like the Deist view that God made the world, just as a watchmaker makes a watch, then wound it up, so that it is now running by its own mechanism. He Himself makes no interruption, no interference, no intrusion into the plane of history.

That is not the God of Scripture. The sovereign God is the Lord of providence, who provides daily for His people and responds to their cries. The laws of the universe are not fixed, immutable, abstract, regulatory principles of inert nature. What we call laws simply refer to the ordinary and normal operations by which the sovereign God runs this planet. And that sovereign God is never at the mercy of His own creation. He is the sovereign God.

The fact that there are intricate mechanisms working in this world does not mean that God has to do an immediate miracle every time we pray for something. God is standing above the world and is orchestrating every molecule in that world, all of the so-called natural, normal, regulating causes. Therefore, God is able to answer prayer without in any way disrupting or interrupting the natural mechanism of the planet.

In fact, when we look at the miracles in the Bible, we see that some of them are wrought immediately—that is, without means, directly—while other miracles are wrought mediately— that is, by virtue of intermediary means. Think of the Israelites' escape from Egypt through the Red Sea. What was miraculous about the parting of the waters of the Red Sea? It's not miraculous for a great wind to blow; that happens all the time. It is certainly extraordinary, but not necessarily miraculous, for the wind to blow with such intensity that it creates a backwash of water in the sea. That has been known to happen without any sense of a miracle taking place. Yes, it was extraordinary, but it wasn't necessarily miraculous.

What was miraculous about the parting of the Red Sea was that it happened on command. Moses held out his staff and the wind rose. The wind blows every day, but it doesn't blow on my command. I can go to the seashore and command the wind to blow, and nothing will happen. Likewise, I can command the wind to cease on a blustery day, and again my words will have no impact whatsoever, but when the wind rose on the Sea of Galilee, Jesus said, "Peace, be still," and the wind stopped (Mark 4:39). That was a miracle. But in the exodus we have means. We have water and we have wind. We have nature operating, but it is operating under the power of supernature, under the command of God in a crisis moment in the personal history of human beings. That's what we mean by the special providential intervention of God to deliver His people. They prayed and God acted without breaking a law of nature. He can break the laws of nature if He needs to, but He doesn't have to do so in order to answer our prayers.

Prayers as Means to God's Ends

James makes a statement that is vital to our practical under-standing of the relationship of God's sovereignty and prayer. It is a statement that haunts me as I consider this question. He said, "You do not have because you do not ask" (4:2). We must not understand reality as God working alone, as God being at center stage while we are mere puppets who have no active involvement in the plan of redemption. That is not Christianity or Calvinism. It's a distortion. God brings to pass His sovereign ends by virtue of earthly and human means. This is the theological concept of concurrence, and it works as much in the arena of prayer as it does in the other areas that we have considered.

What would you think of a farmer who, when the spring comes, sits on his porch in his rocking chair, folds his hands, and says, "Well, I sure hope we have a great harvest this year; I hope that it's the plan of God to give us abundant crops"? He doesn't plow the field. He doesn't plant the seed. He doesn't weed the rows. He sits there and waits for God to deliver him a harvest from heaven. That's not how a farmer works. If a farmer ever did try to "farm" that way, I think it's clear what would happen—his benefit from the hand of God would be zero. We are called to plow our fields. We are called to plant and to water. And this calling applies to our prayers.

It has been quoted a thousand times, that the Bible says, "God helps those who help themselves." Of course, that is not from the Bible. But in a certain sense, the idea is correct. God calls us to work, to plow, to plant, to read, to study, to prepare. We do all of these things, but He brings the growth. What does Paul say? "I planted, Apollos watered, but God gave the increase" (1 Cor. 3:6).

There's a sense in which intercessory prayer, prayer of supplication, is a work. It's certainly a pleasure, but it requires energy and time. God knows what we need before we ask Him, but He requires the work. He knows that we need bread before we ask Him for it, but He requires us to put forth the work of producing the materials by which our bread is given to us. If we lack the benefits of God's hands in our life, it may very well be because we have not asked; we have not put forth the work of entreating Him in prayer.

Keeping Promises in Context

At this point, I need to sound a warning. In our day, many people have rediscovered the power of prayer. This is a good thing; there's nothing more thrilling in the Christian life than to pray specifically, to express a desire, to make a request or a petition to God, and then see Him answer that request specifically and clearly. It's nice to receive what we pray for, but the added benefit is the assurance we gain that God hears our prayers and answers them. However, some carry this to an extreme and jump to the conclusion that prayer is something of a magic wand, that if we do prayer with the right sound, in the right manner, with the right phrases, and in the right posture, God is obligated to answer. The idea seems to be that we have the capacity to coerce God Almighty into doing for us whatever it is we want Him to do, but God is not a celestial bellhop who is on call every time we press the button, just waiting to serve us our every request.

You might reply that the Bible seems to say that God is willing to give us virtually anything we ask for. You might note that Jesus said, "Ask, and it will be given to you; seek, and you will find; knock, and it will be opened to you" (Matt. 7:7). You might recall that Jesus said, "Whatever things you ask in prayer, believing, you will receive" (Matt. 21:22). You might even note that He said, "If two of you agree on earth concerning anything that they ask, it will be done for them by My Father in heaven" (Matt. 18:19).

We must be very careful in our handling of these verses, taking care to interpret them in their context. Think about it—any number of people would like to see a cure for cancer. I'm sure that I could find at least a few people who would agree with me about this, so if two or three of us got together and agreed that a cure for cancer would be good, and then we prayed about it, would God be obligated to answer?

Jesus clearly said, "If two of you agree on earth concerning anything . . . it will be done," but He made this statement in the context of a vast amount of information about authentic prayer that He had already given to His disciples. We cannot simply come to a text and pick out a verse without examining all of the qualifications our Lord gave in His full teaching of prayer. To do so is to risk ending up with a magical view of the matter.

One of the reasons we're drawn into superstition and ungodly practices is that we are creatures of time. As a result of that fact, we're anxious. We don't know what tomorrow is going to bring. My first prayer as a child was: "Now I lay me down to sleep. I pray the Lord my soul to keep. If I should die before I wake, I pray the Lord my soul to take." That last sentence always scared me, the part about dying before I woke up. I didn't know whether I was going to die before I would wake. Actually, not much has changed since then. I don't know what this afternoon is going to bring into my life. I don't know what tomorrow, next week, or next year is going to bring into my life, and neither do you. We live always on the edge of eternity, as finite creatures. And that puts anxiety into our souls.

Isn't it interesting that one of the most lucrative businesses in the United States of America in the twenty-first century, a time of great educational advance, a day of exploding knowledge, continues to be the practice of astrology. I've said many times, I could ask my seminary students to name the twelve tribes of Israel, and I'd be very happy if they could name eight or nine. But I could ask them to name the twelve signs of the zodiac, and virtually every one of them, given enough time, could name all twelve. I don't think that meant they were more into astrology than biblical history, but it did suggest that astrology is a phenomenon that is widespread in our culture. Why? Because we want to know the future.

That is not what living in Christian faith is all about. My tomorrow and your tomorrows are in the hands of God. We make our requests before Him and we trust our tomorrows to His sovereignty. I'm delighted that my future is not in the hands of the stars or the soothsayers. Rather, my future is in the hands of the will of the sovereign God.

INDEX OF SUBJECTS AND NAMES

INDEX OF SCRIPTURE

ABOUT THE AUTHOR

Dr. R.C. Sproul was founder of Ligonier Ministries, founding pastor of Saint Andrew's Chapel in Sanford, Fla., first president of Reformation Bible College, and executive editor of *Tabletalk* magazine. His radio program, *Renewing Your Mind*, is still broadcast daily on hundreds of radio stations around the world and can also be heard online. He was author of more than one hundred books, including *The Holiness of God*, *Chosen by God*, and *Everyone's a Theologian*. He was recognized throughout the world for his articulate defense of the inerrancy of Scripture and the need for God's people to stand with conviction upon His Word.